MOST THIS AMAZING DAY

AN ANTHOLOGY OF SPIRITUAL VERSE

Nigel Watts

Fount
An Imprint of HarperCollins*Publishers*

Fount Paperbacks is an Imprint of
HarperCollins*Religious*
Part of HarperCollins*Publishers*
77–85 Fulham Palace Road, London w6 8jb

First published in Great Britain in 1998 by HarperCollins*Religious*
1 3 5 7 9 10 8 6 4 2

ISBN 0 00 628062 5

Printed and bound in Great Britain by
Woolnough Bookbinding Ltd, Irthlingborough, Northamptonshire

CONTENTS

———

———

INTRODUCTION

———

The poems in this collection were suggested by over 100 prominent artists, thinkers, writers, politicians and entertainers. Some respondents are 'professionally' religious, some would describe themselves as atheists: all are people who, in their different ways, have ascribed significance to matters of the spirit in their own lives. I asked two questions of each person: 'Do you have a favourite poem that expresses an aspect of your spiritual experience (whatever that may mean to you)?' And 'Why does the poem mean something to you?' The results are what you see.

Why bother with an anthology of poetry? Because, even leaving aside the pleasure which poetry can bring, a poem is a remarkable thing. Freed from the novel's need to tell a story, or the essay's need to make sense, a poem can provide the reader with an experience which no other use of words can achieve. Reaching behind the rational mind, poets can bring forth those strange, neither-flesh-nor-fish creatures, metaphors. A metaphor does not compute, it makes no sense – it is *non*sense. The moon is not at all like a balloon: it is a billion times bigger; it is made of rock, not rubber; it is a satellite of a planet, not a child's toy. But of course, sometimes only nonsense can do the job of capturing a living experience in the net of words. Because the moon *is* very much like a balloon when you lie on your back in a darkened garden and rest it in the cup of your outstretched hands.

In a way, only a metaphor can come close to doing justice to the essence of that which it tries to describe, particularly the abstract qualities which we are so concerned with. A scientist may do well in describing the moon in terms of mass and composition. However, the search for meaning and the exploration of feeling and death and emotion – those things that we forever try to understand – *those* things are closer to the reach of poets, with their messy, irrational thinking.

A few respondents complained about the poor grammar of the title of this anthology, *Most This Amazing Day*. But in a way only poor grammar and illogic stand a chance of doing justice to the amazing-ness of the day. ('To amaze' originally meant 'to astound, bewilder, perplex', or as the philosopher Alan Watts put it, 'to be lost in a maze'.) The title, by the way, is from the opening of an E. E. Cummings poem: 'i thank You God for most this amazing/ day'.

Why bother with an anthology of *spiritual* poetry? Because spiritual poetry can reach into our hearts in a way which dry dogma can never do. The understanding, or comfort, or inspiration that many of us seek from words is often more forthcoming from poetry than from anywhere else. One of our greatest teachers was also a great improvisational poet: 'Consider the lilies,' he once said.

But what do I mean by 'spirit'? I have come across no more succinct or accurate definition than that of Maya Angelou: 'Spirit is an invisible force made visible in all life.' Poets come into their own here, because they know that any name they give to this invisible force is just a sign, an approximation, a groping to define the indefinable. Words point to things; they are not the things themselves. Believing that the word 'God' is the thing itself is like believing that a printed menu is the food. Though many of the poets in this collection employ traditional religious terms (such as 'God', 'Lord', 'Jesus', 'soul' and 'spirit'), most, I imagine, would agree with what Czeslaw Milosz says in his poem 'Meditation': 'Lord, it is quite possible that people, while praising you, were mistaken.'

If God is not 'a ruler on a throne', then what is he? A feeling, perhaps, such as love. 'Love me brought/ And love me wrought' begins the anonymous poem 'Christ's Love-Song'. Nowhere is love more eloquently spoken of than in George Herbert's poem of the same name. Here, as Ludovic Kennedy points out, the word 'love' is surely a synonym for God.

Rilke's vision is more turbulent: he uses the image of a storm to describe the spirit, the 'shifter of shapes', while Shelley, a Platonist, employs the epic simile of the wild west wind:

> Wild Spirit, which art moving everywhere;
> Destroyer and preserver; hear, O hear!

Sometimes the experience of the spirit is personalized, as with the Sufi poets Shabistari and Hafiz, who call it the Self or the Friend or the Beloved, while

Goethe's beautiful phrase is 'the sacred open mystery'. The Vietnamese Buddhist monk, Thich Nhat Hanh, sees the signs of the invisible force made visible wherever he looks – in ugliness and cruelty as well as beauty. Lao Tzu hesitates to play the naming game: 'Existence is beyond the power of words to define,' he says. If a name is needed, he says, let the name be '*wonder*'.

There is a Sufi story of a group of people falling out over how to spend their money: some want to buy *angur*, others want *inab*, yet others want *uzum*. Of course, they are arguing about the same thing without realizing it; the words they use all mean 'grapes' in their own language. It is not the word that counts, but the experience; not the label but the taste on the tongue. And whether the tongue belongs to one who, in the words of Brian Aldiss, has 'sought to disbelieve', or one who finds their spiritual home in religion, the experience is no less valid. What one may gropingly call 'God' another may gropingly call 'Life'. It is therefore important to regard this as an anthology of *spiritual* poetry, rather than *religious* poetry. For though spirituality is to be found at the heart of religion, it is not confined to religion. Spirituality casts a broad net: theism, atheism, agnosticism, and the world-view that neither affirms nor denies these beliefs. All can be included within spirituality, for though faith and worship may be part of it, they are not demanded. Some of these poems, taken alone, may not seem particularly spiritual. Seen in context, however, I believe they all, in their own way, address the 'invisible force'. This force, whether disguised as nature, or death, or human emotions has been the main concern of poets throughout the ages. This force is what we struggle to under-stand, what we find ourselves immersed in, the medium in which we can sometimes discover the 'who' of who we are.

Though these poems are presented alphabetically by nominator, they could as easily be grouped according to subject matter. There are many poems about death, the 'inevitable hour' when we have no choice but to address this force. Within this group there are quietly desolate poems about mortality, such as Sarah Churchill's epitaph for her father, Winston Churchill; the poem written by Dana Gioia upon his young son's death; the poignant W. B. Yeats poem, 'When You are Old'. There are sobering reminders of the transitory nature of temporal power in Shelley's 'Ozyman-dias', chosen by Alan Clarke. And there are poems in which death becomes a doorway to something else, where grief, as Elizabeth Jennings says, 'begins to flower/ Into a new love'.

A second grouping of poems is around the theme of spirit in matter. Perhaps one of the greatest such poems appears in this anthology: Walt Whitman's epic 'I Sing the Body Electric', nominated by Steven Berkoff:

> The man's body is sacred, and the woman's body is sacred;
> No matter who it is, it is sacred.

This is the essence of the mystic vision: the experience of spirit as immanent rather than transcendent – not separate from the physical world but, as Wordsworth puts it, 'far more deeply interfused' than we could possibly imagine. The mystical poet has a peculiar problem: words, which are at the best of times inadequate, completely fail him now. The mystic's world does not behave in neat Newtonian ways: definitions slip and slide; surface appearances are seen as masking a deeper divinity; our intellect fails. As Thomas Traherne sings in 'Wonder':

> I within did flow
> With seas of life, like wine;
> I nothing in the world did know,
> But 'twas divine.

When you no longer know anything, then you can KNOW. And when you open your mouth, don't be surprised if beautiful nonsense comes out. Michael Horovitz, in a poem dedicated to his wife, refers to 'this super-natural/ real world', while Eli Jaxon-Bear, writing about *his* wife, the spiritual teacher Gangaji, conjures an image that is precise, lovely ... and impossible:

> So sing sweetly
> my love,
> my earthen vessel
> of light.

Perhaps the most striking of the poems that celebrate the sacred made flesh is 'Beatitude' by Claire Bateman, no less so for being nominated by the monk and hermit, Brother Steindl-Rast. Here, sex is a sacrament, even between those of us who are most vulnerably human:

Blessed are the flabby people at Walgreen's
buying Trojan transparent ribbed golden condoms.

A related cluster of poems are those which address what in psychological terms
might be called the 'shadow'. Robert Browning in 'Pisgah-Sights 1' embraces
the shadow as the inevitable other side of light:

Roughness and smoothness,
Shine and defilement,
Grace and uncouthness:
One reconcilement.

'The Seventh Angel' by Zbigniew Herbert likewise seeks no apology for the
reprobate angel who

is black and nervous
and has been fined many times for
illegal import of sinners.

Like it or not, we are in the world. We have bodies; those bodies have urges,
appetites. We have minds, sometimes full of anger and cruelty and greed.
Don't banish your negative thoughts, the Sufi master Rumi says in 'The
Guesthouse', even though they may wreck your home. Welcome them like
honoured guests, for each of them bears a gift.
    Though many religions have taught that our shadowy aspects are a cause
for us to hang our heads in shame, George Herbert will have none of that.
In one of his greatest poems, 'Love', he combines those two qualities which
characterize the metaphysical poet: irresistible logic and a swooning heart. We
are the creation of Love, he says; our sins are borne by Christ, and we deserve
to take our place at the feast of life.
    We will doubtless fall short of our own – and others' – standards, and yet
we fall only to rise. In 'The Visit and the Gift' we find these wonderful lines:

Sometimes, from sheer habit,
I'm back on the compost heap.
And sometimes,

when that glance finds me again,
I am back in the Rose Garden.

Once we are back in the Garden, what is there to do but to bend our knee, like the cattle in Thomas Hardy's poem, 'The Oxen'?

Some of the verses in this collection have been sung as hymns, and others have been recited as prayers. There is another category, however, where no such knee-bending takes place. There is the extraordinary image in the Czeslaw Milosz poem, 'Meditation', of God not as someone sitting upon a throne, but as a wanderer camping by 'invisible waters', watching thoughtfully, shaking his head.

Sometimes God is absent and we hear only our echo. Sometimes we have to wrestle with angels. Even if we are kneeling, it is often more in hope than in expectation, and the unseen wings we hear in the high roof of the church are 'bats not angels', as in the R. S. Thomas poem, 'In a Country Church'.

We may all shake our fists at times at these invisible forces. But hopefully, like George Herbert, our tantrum is as transitory as that of a petulant child. The two most arresting words that appear in this collection are, for me, those that conclude 'The Collar', nominated by Stephen Fry. After railing at God and threatening to storm off, the speaker reports:

But as I raved and grew more fierce and wild
At every word,
Me thought I heard one calling, *Child!*
And I replied, *My Lord.*

Regardless of subject matter or theme, of all the metaphors for the spirit that are used, by far the most common is *light*. God is the 'great Sun', Charles Causley says. John Henry Newman prays for a guiding beacon in 'Lead Kindly Light', and Robert Pirsig's commentary on this poem makes clear the prevalence of light imagery across different cultures. The Irish poet and scholar Sedulius Scottus proclaims, 'Last night did Christ the Sun rise'. Shabistari talks to the moon, Henry Vaughan sees the saints as shining lights.

Just as the divine domain is often spoken of in terms of light, so the human condition is often likened to darkness. 'Make light my shadow; kindle/ my fear with radiant, heavenly shafts', James Strecker pleads in 'Coltrane's Prayer'. Kathleen Raine's poem 'Night Sky' begins:

> There came such clear opening of the night sky,
> The deep glass of wonders, the dark mind
> In unclouded gaze of the abyss
> Opened like the expression of a face.

The dispelling of the darkness – if it ever comes – is the moment of revelation, a moment in which the invisible force becomes visible, just as the inner smile breaks out on a face. Suddenly things stand out, revealed, lit up from a hidden source. 'I have seen the sun break through/ to illuminate a small field', R. S. Thomas writes, capturing this most ineffable of experiences in the most accessible image. The revelation can be as fleeting as the sun on a spring day, and easily dismissed, though, as Thomas says, its transitory brightness presages 'the eternity which awaits you'. Sometimes, however, the enlightenment can be a flooding of the senses when time stops: 'I saw a great light come down over London,/ And buildings and cars and people were still', Jay Ramsay's poem 'transmissions' begins.

When the light is experienced, it is almost always unexpected. Rupert Brooke uses the vivid image of travellers round the camp fire at night singing of seeing 'at some sudden turn'

> Against the black and muttering trees
> Thine altar, wonderfully white,
> Among the forests of the Night.

And this introduces a common element in the poems of revelation – what Robert Tear calls the 'Holy Now'. At the moment of illumination, time falls away. Suddenly free from the burden of the past and the anxiety of the future, we can live in the perpetual present in which everything is new, and joyous for that. I would like to bump into Rabbi Lionel Blue on his way to work, singing, as he does, the refrain from Sydney Carter's hymn: 'And it's from the old I travel to the new/ Keep me travelling along with you.' Not only is everything fresh-minted in these moments out of time, but everything is gloriously significant. The windhover is no longer just a bird, it is Christ himself. And not only the obviously magnificent, but *everything* – even the mundane and previously trivial – becomes full of meaning, and you wake as if from a sleep. This waking comes often as the result of a profound shock – as in Brian Patten's case with the death of his mother. It is then that the veils can fall from our eyes and we can say, even in the midst of grief:

> Good morning dear world,
> So briefly known.
> In flashes only seen,
> So often missed
> By eyes so self-obsessed.

This is a long way from our day-to-day utilitarian thinking. However, there is a further step towards enlightenment, even beyond this awakened state; for there are times when not only is the world new, but it is wonderful. George Herbert, with acute insight, called this witnessing 'heaven in ordinary', when a day is not just another 24 hours of our life, but is *amazing*, and we stutter and sing:

> i thank You God for most this amazing
> day...

This is not just an anthology of spiritual verse, but one of *favourite* spiritual verse. Over 100 people, each with their own relationship with this 'invisible force made visible', have given a gift to us. This is a personal matter: many of these poems have been learned by heart; some have been carried in wallets, written to friends, pinned above writing desks; some have been written by the nominator – a doubly personal contribution. Most of the poems are accompanied by comments. Many of them have been called upon in times of distress, and many of them have been held as precious.

Because favourite poems *are* precious, not as a diamond or a ruby is precious, but as a pebble is precious, a pebble scented with salt and seaweed that we take home at the end of a long day at the seaside. We keep them in a drawer and forget about them until one rainy day we come across them by accident. Then we take them up, marvelling at how perfectly they fit our palm, memories of sun flooding back to us.

There is a special quality to favourite poems, particularly when they are learned by heart. When we read and reread them, they become part of our consciousness, and they are no longer words on the page, but talismans, mantras, prayers even – magical objects with the power to transport us from the busy materialism of our everyday lives to that sunny day on the beach. I hope that in this collection you find some pebbles of your own.

NIGEL WATTS

ACKNOWLEDGEMENTS

———

The following writers and publishers have kindly given permission for the reprinting of copyright material:

'The Path' from *At the Caligula Hotel* by Brian Aldiss (Sinclair Stevenson, 1995). Reprinted by kind permission of Curtis Brown Group Ltd.

'Musée des Beaux-Arts' by W. H. Auden, reprinted by kind permission of Faber and Faber.

Comment on 'The Heart Sutra' taken from the introduction of *Entering the Stream*, compiled and edited by Samuel Bercholz and Sherab Chodzin Kohn (Rider).

'One more step' by Sydney Carter from *Green Print for Song*. Reprinted by kind permission of Stainer & Bell.

'I am the Great Sun' by Charles Causley, from *Collected Poems* (Macmillan Publishers).

'Ithaca' by C. F. Cavafy, translated by Rae Dalven, from *The Complete Poems of C. F. Cavafy* (Chatto & Windus, 1961).

'The Donkey' and 'A Hymn' by G. K. Chesterton, from *Poems for all Purposes – the selected poems of G. K. Chesterton* (Pimlico, 1994). Reprinted by kind permission of A. P. Watt Ltd on behalf of the Royal Literary Fund.

'Please Call me by my True Names', reprinted from *Call Me By My True Names: The Collected Poems of Thich Nhat Hanh* (1993) by Thich Nhat Hanh with kind permission of Parallax Press, Berkeley, California.

'The Seventh Angel' by Zbigniew Herbert, translated by Peter Dale Scott, from *Selected Poems* (Carcanet Press 1985).

'Glad Day', © Michael Horovitz from *Growing Up: selected poems and pictures 1951–1979* (Alison & Busby, 1979).

'Ice Melts My Fire' by Eli Jaxon-Bear, © Eli Jaxon-Bear.

'Into the Hour' by Elizabeth Jennings, from *Collected Poems* (Carcanet Press).

'The Appeal' and 'The Gods of Copybook Headings' by Rudyard Kipling. Reprinted by kind permission of A. P. Watt Ltd on behalf of the National Trust.

'Returning to the Root' from *Lao Tzu: Tao Te Ching*, translated by Ursula K. Le Guin, © 1997. Reprinted by arrangement with Shambhala Publications, Inc., 300 Massachusetts Ave., Boston, MA 02115.

'Bhagavati', © Barry Long. Reprinted by kind permission of Barry Long.

'The Sunlight on the Garden' by Louis MacNeice from *Collected Poems* (Faber, 1979).

'Meditation' by Czeslaw Milosz, translated by Czeslaw Milosz and Robert Hass, from *Provinces: Poems 1987–1991* (Carcanet Press, 1991).

'Full Circle World' by Brian Patten, from *Armada* (HarperCollinsPublishers)

'Night Sky' by Kathleen Raine, from *Collected Poems 1935–1980* (George Allen & Unwin, 1981). Reprinted with kind permission of Kathleen Raine. 'transmissions XXIV' by Jay Ramsay, from *transmissions* (Stride, 1989). Reprinted with kind permission of Jay Ramsay.

'The Man Watching' from *Selected Poems of Rainer Maria Rilke*, edited and translated by Robert Bly, © Robert Bly 1981. Reprinted by kind permission of HarperCollinsPublishers, Inc.

'The Guesthouse' by Jalaluddin Rumi, translation © Maryam Mafi.

'The Visit and the Gift' by Mahmud Shabistari, from *Desert Wisdom: The Middle Eastern Tradition from the Goddess through the Sufis* (Thorsons, London). © 1995 Neil Douglas-Klotz. Reprinted by kind permission of Neil Douglas-Klotz.

'A letter to John Donne' by C. H. Sisson, from *Collected Poems 1943–1983* (Carcanet Press, 1984).

'To the Spirit', © Robert Tear. Reprinted by kind permission of Robert Tear.

'In a Country Church' and 'The Bright Field' by R. S. Thomas from *Collected Poems 1945–1990* (J. M. Dent & Sons).

'Sweetness in Bitterness', © Hüseyin Top, translated by Kayhan Alsaç and Nigel Watts.

'Existence is beyond the power of words to define' by Lao Tzu, translated by Witter Bynner, from *The Way of Life* (Perigee Books, 1994), © the John Day Company Inc.

'Taliesin and the Spring of Vision' by Vernon Watkins from *Selected Poems 1930–1960* (Faber and Faber). Reprinted by kind permission of Gwen Watkins.

'The Silent Self', © Harry Wiggett. Reprinted by kind permission of Harry Wiggett.

'Man and the Echo', 'The Second Coming' and 'When You are Old' by W. B. Yeats, from *The Collected Poems of W. B. Yeats* (J. M. Dent & Sons, 1990). Reprinted by kind permission of A. P. Watt Ltd on behalf of Michael Yeats.

THE WRECK OF THE DEUTSCHLAND

To the
happy memory of five Franciscan nuns
exiles by the Falck Laws
drowned between midnight and morning of
Dec. 7th, 1875

PART THE FIRST

1

Thou mastering me
God! giver of breath and bread;
World's strand, sway of the sea;
Lord of living and dead;
Thou hast bound bones and veins in me, fastened me flesh,
And after it almost unmade, what with dread,
Thy doing: and dost thou touch me afresh?
Over again I feel thy finger and find thee.

2

I did say yes
O at lightning and lashed rod;
Thou heardest me truer than tongue confess
Thy terror, O Christ, O God;
Thou knowest the walls, altar and hour and night:
The swoon of a heart that the sweep and the hurl of thee trod
Hard down with a horror of height:
And the midriff astrain with leaning of, laced with fire of stress.

The frown of his face
Before me, the hurtle of hell
Behind, where, where was a, where was a place?
I whirled out wings that spell
And fled with a fling of the heart to the heart of the Host.
My heart, but you were dovewinged, I can tell,
Carrier-witted, I am bold to boast,
To flash from the flame to the flame then, tower from the grace
to the grace.

I am soft sift
In an hourglass – at the wall
Fast, but mined with a motion, a drift,
And it crowds and it combs to the fall;
I steady as a water in a well, to a poise, to a pane,
But roped with, always, all the way down from the tall
Fells or flanks of the voel,¹ a vein
Of the gospel proffer, a pressure, a principle, Christ's gift.

I kiss my hand
To the stars, lovely-asunder
Starlight, wafting him out of it; and
Glow, glory in thunder;
Kiss my hand to the dappled-with-damson west:
Since, tho' he is under the world's splendour and wonder,
His mystery must be instressed, stressed;
For I greet him the days I meet him, and bless when I understand.

---

¹ voel = bare hill

6

Not out of his bliss
Springs the stress felt
Nor first from heaven (and few know this)
Swings the stroke dealt –
Stroke and a stress that stars and storms deliver,
That guilt is hushed by, hearts are flushed by and melt –
But it rides time like riding a river
(And here the faithful waver, the faithless fable and miss.)

7

It dates from day
Of his going in Galilee;
Warm-laid grave of a womb-life grey;
Manger, maiden's knee;
The dense and the driven Passion, and frightful sweat:
Thence the discharge of it, there its swelling to be,
Though felt before, though in high flood yet –
What none would have known of it, only the heart, being hard
    at bay,

8

Is out with it! Oh,
We lash with the best or worst
Word last! How a lush-kept plush-capped sloe
Will, mouthed to flesh-burst,
Gush! – flush the man, the being with it, sour or sweet
Brim, in a flash, full! – Hither then, last or first,
To hero of Calvary, Christ's feet –
Never ask if meaning it, wanting it, warned of it – men go.

9

Be adored among men,
God, three-numberèd form;
Wring thy rebel, dogged in den,
Man's malice, with wrecking and storm.
Beyond saying sweet, past telling of tongue,
Thou art lightning and love, I found it, a winter and warm;
Father and fondler of heart thou hast wrung:
Hast thy dark descending and most art merciful then.

10

With an anvil-ding
And with fire in him forge thy will
Or rather, rather then, stealing as Spring
Through him, melt him but master him still:
Whether at once, as once at a crash Paul,
Or as Austin,[2] a lingering-out sweet skill,
Make mercy in all of us, out of us all
Mastery, but be adored, but be adored King.

---

[2] Austin = St Augustine of Hippo (AD 354–430)

11

'Some find me a sword; some
The flange and the rail; flame,
Fang, or flood' goes Death on drum,
And storms bugle his fame.
But we dream we are rooted in earth – Dust!
Flesh falls within sight of us, we, though our flower the same,
Wave with the meadow, forget that there must
The sour scythe cringe, and the blear share come.

12

On Saturday sailed from Bremen,
American-outward-bound,
Take settler and seamen, tell men with women,
Two hundred souls in the round –
O Father, not under thy feathers nor ever as guessing
The goal was a shoal, of a fourth the doom to be drowned;
Yet did the dark side of the bay of thy blessing
Not vault them, the millions of rounds of thy mercy not reeve [3]
even them in?

---

[3] reeve = rope together

Into the snows she sweeps,
    Hurling the haven behind,
The Deutschland, on Sunday; and so the sky keeps,
    For the infinite air is unkind,
And the sea flint-flake, black-backed in the regular blow,
Sitting Eastnortheast, in cursed quarter, the wind;
    Wiry and white-fiery and whirlwind-swivellèd snow
Spins to the widow-making unchilding unfathering deeps.

14

She drove in the dark to leeward,
    She struck – not a reef or a rock
But the combs of a smother of sand: night drew her
    Dead to the Kentish Knock;
And she beat the bank down with her bows and the ride of
    her keel:
The breakers rolled on her beam with ruinous shock;
    And canvas and compass, the whorl and the wheel
Idle for ever to waft her or wind her with, these she endured.

15

Hope had grown grey hairs,
    Hope had mourning on,
Trenched with tears, carved with cares,
    Hope was twelve hours gone;
And frightful a nightfall folded rueful a day
Nor rescue, only rocket and lightship, shone,
    And lives at last were washing away:
To the shrouds they took, – they shook in the hurling and horrible airs.

One stirred from the rigging to save
The wild woman-kind below,
With a rope's end round the man, handy and brave –
He was pitched to his death at a blow,
For all his dreadnought breast and braids of thew:[4]
They could tell him for hours, dandled the to and fro
Through the cobbled foam-fleece. What could he do
With the burl of the fountains of air, buck and the flood of the wave?

They fought with God's cold –
And they could not and fell to the deck
(Crushed them) or water (and drowned them) or rolled
With the sea-romp over the wreck.
Night roared, with the heart-break hearing a heart-broke rabble,
The woman's wailing, the crying of child without check –
Till a lioness arose breasting the babble,
A prophetess towered in the tumult, a virginal tongue told.

Ah, touched in your bower of bone,
Are you! turned for an exquisite smart,
Have you! make words break from me here all alone,
Do you! – mother of being in me, heart.
O unteachably after evil, but uttering truth,
Why tears? is it? tears; such a melting, a madrigal start!
Never-eldering revel and river of youth,
What can it be, this glee? the good you have there of your own?

---

[4] thew = muscles

Sister, a sister calling
    A master, her master and mine! –
And the inboard seas run swirling and hawling;
    The rash smart sloggering brine
  Blinds her; but she that weather sees one thing, one;
  Has one fetch in her: she rears herself to divine
    Ears, and the call of the tall nun
To the men in the tops and the tackle rode over the storm's brawling.

20

She was first of a five and came
    Of a coifèd sisterhood.
(O Deutschland, double a desperate name!
    O world wide of its good!
  But Gertrude,[5] lily and Luther, are two of a town.
  Christ's lily, and beast of the waste wood:
    From life's dawn it is drawn down,
Abel is Cain's brother and breasts they have sucked the same.)

21

Loathed for a love men know in them,
    Banned by the land of their birth,
  Rhine refused them. Thames would ruin them;
    Surf, snow, river and earth
  Gnashed: but thou art above, thou Orion of light;
  Thy unchancelling poising palms were weighing the worth,
    Thou martyr-master: in thy sight
Storm flakes were scroll-leaved flowers, lily showers – sweet heaven was astrew
    in them.

---

[5] Gertrude = a Catholic saint of Eisleben, the birthplace of Luther.

Five! the finding and sake
And cipher of suffering Christ.
Mark, the mark is of man's make
And the word of it Sacrificed.
But he scores it in scarlet himself on his own bespoken,
Before-time-taken, dearest prizèd and priced –
Stigma, signal, cinquefoil token
For lettering of the lamb's fleece, ruddying of the rose-flake.

Joy fall to thee, father Francis,
Drawn to the Life that died;
With the gnarls of the nails in thee, niche of the lance, his
Lovescape crucified
And seal of his seraph-arrival! and these thy daughters
And five-livèd and leavèd favour and pride,
Are sisterly sealed in wild waters,
To bathe in his fall-gold mercies, to breathe in his all-fire glances.

Away in the loveable west,
On a pastoral forehead of Wales,
I was under a roof here, I was at rest,
And they the prey of the gales;
She to the black-about air, to the breaker, the thickly
Falling flakes, to the throng that catches and quails
Was calling 'O Christ, Christ, come quickly':
The cross to her she calls Christ to her, christens her wild-worst Best.

The majesty! what did she mean?
Breathe, arch and original Breath.
Is it love in her of the being as her lover had been?
Breathe, body of lovely Death.
They were else-minded then, altogether, the men
Woke thee with a *we are perishing* in the weather of Gennesareth.
Or is it that she cried for the crown then,
The keener to come at the comfort for feeling the combating keen?

For how to the heart's cheering
The down-dugged ground-hugged grey
Hovers off, the jay-blue heavens appearing
Of pied and peeled May!
Blue-beating and hoary-glow height; or night, still higher,
With belled fire and the moth-soft Milky Way,
What by your measure is the heaven of desire,
The treasure never eyesight got, nor was ever guessed what for the hearing?

No, but it was not these.
The jading and jar of the cart,
Time's tasking, it is fathers that asking for ease
Of the sodden-with-its-sorrowing heart,
Not danger, electrical horror; then further it finds
The appealing of the Passion is tenderer in prayer apart:
Other, I gather, in measure her mind's
Burden, in wind's burly and beat of endragonèd seas.

But how shall I ... make me room there:
　　Reach me a ... Fancy, come faster –
　Strike you the sight of it? look at it loom there,
　　Thing that she ... There then! the Master,
Ipse, the only one, Christ, King, Head:
　He was to cure the extremity where he had cast her;
　　Do, deal, lord it with living and dead;
Let him ride, her pride, in his triumph, despatch and have done with his doom
　　there.

　　Ah! there was a heart right!
　　　There was single eye!
　Read the unshapeable shock night
　　And knew the who and the why;
Wording it how but by him that present and past,
Heaven and earth are word of, worded by? –
　The Simon Peter of a soul! to the blast
Tarpeian-fast, but a blown beacon of light.

　　Jesu, heart's light,
　　　Jesu, maid's son,
　What was the feast followed the night
　　Thou hadst glory of this nun? –
Feast of the one woman without stain.
For so conceivèd, so to conceive thee is done;
　But here was heart-throe, birth of a brain,
Word, that heard and kept thee and uttered thee outright.

Well, she has thee for the pain, for the
   Patience; but pity of the rest of them!
  Heart, go and bleed at a bitterer vein for the
    Comfortless unconfessed of them –
No not uncomforted: lovely-felicitous Providence
Finger of a tender of, O of a feathery delicacy, the breast of the
   Maiden could obey so, be a bell to, ring of it, and
Startle the poor sheep back! is the shipwrack then a harvest, does tempest carry
   the grain for thee?

I admire thee, master of the tides,
   Of the Yore-flood, of the year's fall;
  The recurb and the recovery of the gulf's sides,
    The girth of it and the wharf of it and the wall;
Stanching, quenching ocean of a motionable mind;
Ground of being, and granite of it: past all
   Grasp God, throned behind
Death with a sovereignty that heeds but hides, bodes but abides;

With a mercy that outrides
   The all of water, an ark
  For the listener; for the lingerer with a love glides
    Lower than death and the dark;
A vein for the visiting of the past-prayer, pent in prison,
The-last-breath penitent spirits – the uttermost mark
   Our passion-plungèd giant risen,
The Christ of the Father compassionate, fetched in the storm of his strides.

Now burn, new born to the world,
 Double-naturèd Name,
The heaven-flung, heart-fleshed, maiden-furled
 Miracle-in-Mary-of-flame,
Mid-numberèd He in three of the thunder-throne!
Not a dooms-day dazzle in his coming nor dark as he came;
 Kind, but royally reclaiming his own;
A released shower, let flash to the shire, not a lightning of fire hard-hurled.

35

Dame, at our door
 Drowned, and among our shoals.
Remember us in the roads, the heaven-haven of the Reward:
 Our King back, oh, upon English souls!
Let him easter in us, be a dayspring to the dimness of us, be a crimson-
 cresseted east,
More brightening her, rare-dear Britain, as his reign rolls,
 Pride, rose, prince, hero of us, high-priest,
Our hearts' charity hearth's fire, our thoughts' chivalry's throng's Lord.

Gerard Manley Hopkins

Chosen by **the Revd Paul Abram**, Chaplain HM Tower of London: 'The first verse especially makes clear the presence of God in any situation and in every place. My ministry as an Army chaplain has taken me to many countries, usually with young people far from home, so often I have felt the awe of God and the "finger" of God.'

Also chosen by **Cardinal Cahal B. Daly**, Archbishop Emeritus of Armagh: 'I like this poem because of its profound sense of the mystery which is God and the mystery of the suffering of the innocent. The whole poem, and stanzas 5 and 9 in particular, seem to me to speak very directly to the Christian, struggling with the difficulty of reconciling God's loving kindness with the appalling evils of our time, notably Auschwitz, Cambodia, Rwanda. With full awareness of the reality of evil and the mystery of God's allowing it to happen, Hopkins sees, as it were, darkly through the storm and the spray, God's love and mercy.'

THE PATH

O Lord, I reach the gateway of old age,
    Look upon me.
As I stand now in your draughty forecourt
    Look upon me
In my bewilderment. Preserve in me
A late ambition to be wise. Forgive
My sins, my cowardice, my blindness. Save
Me from a righteous rage to denigrate
Those follies which I once myself enjoyed.
Lend me support to aid me on my way
To that more dreadful gate I have to go
Through, unafraid, whenever you decide.

O Lord, in whom I've sought to disbelieve,
    Look upon me.
Fortify an atheist's lack of faith.
    Look upon me.
Greyer, older, that as faculties
Decay and fade I shed my self-regard.
Lord lift this burden of my character
I've had to shoulder all my years. At last
I near the final step. Then may I make
No special claims, that all those whom I love
May not by fears be shamed – remembering
They too must travel down the path I tread.

Brian Aldiss

Chosen by **Brian Aldiss OBE**, writer, poet and critic: 'The confusions of religious and non-religious come to a head as one grows towards the end of life. I hope my poem expresses what many people feel: people who continue to pray to a god to whom they can no longer offer belief.'

THE SONG OF THE PILGRIMS

(Halted around the fire by night, after moon-set, they sing this beneath the trees.)

What light of unremembered skies
Hast thou relumed within our eyes,
Thou whom we seek, whom we shall find?...
A certain odour on the wind,
Thy hidden face beyond the west,
These things have called us; on a quest
Older than any road we trod,
More endless than desire....
        Far God,
Sigh with thy cruel voice, that fills
The soul with longing for dim hills
And faint horizons! For there come
Grey moments of the antient dumb
Sickness of travel, when no song
Can cheer us; but the way seems long;
And one remembers....
        Ah! the beat
Of weary unreturning feet,
And songs of pilgrims unreturning!...
The fires we left are always burning
On the old shrines of home. Our kin
Have built them temples, and therein
Pray to the Gods we know; and dwell
In little houses lovable,
Being happy (we remember how!)
And peaceful even to death....
        O Thou,
God of all long desirous roaming,
Our hearts are sick of fruitless homing,
And crying after lost desire.
Hearten us onward! as with fire
Consuming dreams of other bliss.

The best Thou givest, giving this
Sufficient thing – to travel still
Over the plain, beyond the hill,
Unhesitating through the shade,
Amid the silence unafraid,
Till, at some sudden turn, one sees
Against the black and muttering trees
Thine altar, wonderfully white,
Among the Forests of the Night.

Rupert Brooke

Chosen by **Mary Archer**, scientist: 'The First World War poet, Rupert Brooke, lodged in our house, The Old Vicarage, Grantchester, in the period 1910–12, so his poetry has come to mean a good deal to the family.'

THE DAY IS DONE

The day is done, and the darkness
    Falls from the wings of Night,
As a feather is wafted downward
    From an eagle in his flight.

I see the lights of the village
    Gleam through the rain and the mist,
And a feeling of sadness comes o'er me
    That my soul cannot resist:

A feeling of sadness and longing,
    That is not akin to pain,
And resembles sorrow only
    As the mist resembles the rain.

Come, read to me some poem,
    Some simple and heartfelt lay,
That shall soothe this restless feeling,
    And banish the thoughts of day.

Not from the grand old masters,
    Not from the bards sublime,
Whose distant footsteps echo
    Through the corridors of Time.

For, like the strains of martial music,
    Their mighty thoughts suggest
Life's endless toil and endeavour;
    And tonight I long for rest.

Read from some humbler poet,
    Whose songs gushed from his heart,
As showers from the clouds of summer,
    Or tears from the eyelids start;

Who, through long days of labour,
  And nights devoid of ease,
Still heard in his soul the music
  Of wonderful melodies.

Such songs have power to quiet
  The restless pulse of care,
And come like the benediction
  That follows after prayer.

Then read from the treasured volume
  The poem of thy choice,
And lend to the rhyme of the poet
  The beauty of thy voice.

And the night shall be filled with music,
  And the cares that infest the day
Shall fold their tents, like the Arabs,
  And as silently steal away.

Henry Wadsworth Longfellow

Chosen by **Michael Aspel**, broadcaster: 'When things are going badly, and show no signs of getting better, recalling the last verse of this poem is much more therapeutic than gritting the teeth and counting to ten.'

UNTITLED

We apprehend Him in the alternate voids and fulnesses of a cathedral; in the space that separates the salient features of a picture; in the living geometry of a flower, a seashell, an animal; in the pauses and intervals between notes of music, in their difference and sonority; and, finally, on the plane of conduct, in the love and gentleness, the confidence and humility, which give beauty to the relationship between human beings.

Aldous Huxley

Chosen by **George Baker**, actor and writer: 'This is not a poem in the strict sense of the word but I find it very moving, and once you have read it there is not a blade of grass, a church bell or a greenfinch that doesn't suggest the spirit of God.'

I AM THE GREAT SUN

From a Normandy crucifix of 1632

I am the great sun, but you do not see me,
   I am your husband, but you turn away.
I am the captive, but you do not free me,
   I am the captain you will not obey.

I am the truth, but you will not believe me,
   I am the city where you will not stay,
I am your wife, your child, but you will leave me,
   I am that God to whom you will not pray.

I am your counsel, but you do not hear me,
   I am the lover whom you will betray,
I am the victor, but you do not cheer me,
   I am the holy dove whom you will slay.

I am your life, but if you will not name me,
   Seal up your soul with tears, and never blame me.

Charles Causley

Chosen by **Joan Bakewell**, writer and broadcaster: 'The title says "From a Normandy crucifix". I know these churches of northern France and their melancholy cherubs. Gauguin painted some of those he knew in Brittany. They have a sense of fragrant regret at being rejected by the world. This poem moves me deeply: it reminds me that at every moment of life we can choose to reject or embrace that which is good. Its final couplet is a ringing statement of our individual spiritual responsibility.'

IN PRAISE OF PEACE

Peace is the chief of all the world's wealth,
    And to the heaven it leadeth eke the way;
Peace is of man's soul and life the health,
    And doth with pestilence and war away.
    My liege lord, take heed of what I say,
If war may be left off, take peace on hand,
Which may not be unless God doth it send.

With peace may every creature dwell at rest;
    Without peace there may no life be glad;
Above all other good peace is the best;
    Peace hath himself when war is all bestead;
    Peace is secure, war ever is adread;
Peace is of all charity the key,
That hath the life and soul for to weigh.

For honour vain, or for the world's good,
    They that aforetimes the strong battles made,
Where be they now? – bethink well in thy mood!
    The day is gone, the night is dark and fade,
    Their cruelty which then did make them glad,
They sorrow now, and yet have nought the more;
The blood is shed, which no man may restore.

War is the mother of the wrongs all;
    It slayeth the priest in holy church at mass,
Forliths the maid, and doth her flower to fall;
    The war maketh the great city less,
    And doth the law its rules to overpass,
There is no thing whereof mischief may grow,
Which is not caused by the war, I trow.

John Gower (1399, to Henry IV)

Chosen by **Tony Benn MP**: 'Why do I find this poem meaningful? Because war is a crime against humanity.'

I SING THE BODY ELECTRIC

1

I sing the Body electric;
The armies of those I love engirth me, and I engirth them;
They will not let me off till I go with them, respond to them,
And discorrupt them, and charge them full
    with the charge of the Soul.

2

Was it doubted that those who corrupt their own bodies
    conceal themselves?
And if those who defile the living are as bad
    as they who defile the dead?
And if the body does not do as much as the Soul?
And if the body were not the Soul, what is the Soul?

3

The love of the Body of man or woman balks account –
    the body itself balks account;
That of the male is perfect, that of the female is perfect.

4

The expression of the face balks account;
But the expression of a well-made man
    appears not only in his face;
It is in his limbs and joints also, it is curiously in the joints
    of his hips and wrists;
It is in his walk, the carriage of his neck,
    the flex of his waist and knees – dress does not hide him;
The strong, sweet, supple quality he has,
    strikes through the cotton and flannel;

To see him pass conveys as much as the best poem,
    perhaps more;
You linger to see his back, and the back of his neck
    and shoulder-side.

5

The sprawl and fullness of babes, the bosoms and heads of women,
    the folds of their dress, their style as we pass in the street,
    the contour of their shape downwards,
The swimmer naked in the swimming-bath,
    seen as he swims through the transparent green-shine, or lies with his face up,
    and rolls silently to and fro in the heave of the water,
The bending forward and backward of rowers in rowboats –
    the horseman in his saddle,
Girls, mothers, house-keepers, in all their performances,
The group of labourers seated at noon-time with their open dinner-kettles,
    and their wives waiting,
The female soothing a child –
    the farmer's daughter in the garden or cow-yard,
The young fellow hoeing corn –
    the sleigh-driver guiding his six horses through the crowd,
The wrestle of wrestlers, two apprentice-boys,
    quite grown, lusty, good-natured, native-born,
    out on the vacant lot at sun-down, after work,
The coats and caps thrown down, the embrace of love and resistance,
The upper-hold and under-hold,
    the hair rumpled over and blinding the eyes;
The march of firemen in their own costumes, the play of masculine muscle
    through clean-setting trowsers and waist-straps,
The slow return from the fire,
    the pause when the bell strikes suddenly again,
    and the listening on the alert,
The natural, perfect, varied attitudes –
    the bent head, the curv'd neck, and the counting;
Such-like I love – I loosen myself, pass freely,

am at the mother's breast with the little child,
Swim with the swimmers, wrestle with wrestlers,
	march in line with the firemen, and pause, listen, and count.

6

I knew a man, a common farmer – the father of five sons;
And in them were the fathers of sons –
	and in them were the fathers of sons.

7

This man was of wonderful vigour, calmness, beauty of person;
The shape of his head, the pale yellow and white of his hair and beard,
	and the immeasurable meaning of his black eyes –
	the richness and breadth of his manners,
These I used to go and visit him to see – he was wise also;
He was six feet tall, he was over eighty years old –
	his sons were massive, clean, bearded, tan-faced, handsome;
They and his daughters loved him – all who saw him loved him;
They did not love him by allowance – they loved him with personal love;
He drank water only – the blood show'd like scarlet
	through the clear-brown skin of his face;
He was a frequent gunner and fisher – he sail'd his boat himself –
	he had a fine one presented to him by a ship-joiner –
	he had fowling-pieces, presented to him by men that loved him;
When he went with his five sons and many grand-sons to hunt or fish,
	you would pick him out as the most beautiful and vigorous of the gang,
You would wish long and long to be with him – you would wish
	to sit by him in the boat, that you and he might touch each other.

8

I have perceiv'd that to be with those I like is enough,
To stop in company with the rest at evening is enough,
To be surrounded by beautiful, curious, breathing, laughing flesh
    is enough,
To pass among them, or touch any one, or rest my arm ever so lightly
    round his or her neck for a moment – what is this, then?
I do not ask any more delight – I swim in it, as in a sea.

9

There is something in staying close to men and women,
    and looking on them, and in the contact and odour of them,
    that pleases the soul well;
All things please the soul – but these please the soul well.

10

This is the female form;
A divine nimbus exhales from it from head to foot;
It attracts with fierce undeniable attraction!
I am drawn by its breath as if I were no more than a helpless vapour –
    all falls aside but myself and it;
Books, art, religion, time, the visible and solid earth,
    the atmosphere and the clouds, and what was expected of heaven
    or fear'd of hell, are now consumed;
Mad filaments, ungovernable shoots play out of it –
    the response likewise ungovernable;
Hair, bosom, hips, bend of legs, negligent falling hands, all diffused –
    mine too diffused;
Ebb stung by the flow, and flow stung by the ebb –
    love-flesh swelling and deliciously aching;
Limitless limpid jets of love hot and enormous, quivering jelly of love,
    white-blow and delirious juice;
Bridegroom night of love, working surely and softly into the prostrate dawn;

Undulating into the willing and yielding day,
Lost in the cleave of the clasping and sweet-flesh'd day.

11

This is the nucleus – after the child is born of woman,
    the man is born of woman;
This is the bath of birth – this is the merge of small and large,
    and the outlet again.

12

Be not ashamed, women – your privilege encloses the rest,
    and is the exit of the rest;
You are the gates of the body, and you are the gates of the soul.

13

The female contains all qualities, and tempers them –
    she is in her place, and moves with perfect balance;
She is all things duly veil'd – she is both passive and active;
She is to conceive daughters as well as sons,
    and sons as well as daughters.

14

As I see my soul reflected in nature;
As I see through a mist, one with inexpressible
    completeness and beauty,
See the bent head, and arms folded over the breast –
    the female I see.

15

The male is not less the soul, nor more – he too is in his place;
He too is all qualities – he is action and power;
The flush of the known universe is in him;
Scorn becomes him well, and appetite and defiance
    become him well;
The wildest largest passions, bliss that is utmost, sorrow that is utmost,
    become him well – pride is for him;
The full-spread pride of man is calming and excellent to the soul;
Knowledge becomes him – he likes it always –
    he brings everything to the test of himself;
Whatever the survey, whatever the sea and the sail,
    he strikes soundings at last only here;
(Where else does he strike soundings, except here?)

16

The man's body is sacred, and the woman's body is sacred;
No matter who it is, it is sacred;
Is it a slave? Is it one of the dull-faced immigrants
    just landed on the wharf?
Each belongs here or anywhere, just as much as the well-off –
    just as much as you;
Each has his or her place in the procession.

17

(All is a procession;
The universe is a procession, with measured and beautiful motion.)

18

Do you know so much yourself, that you call the slave
    or the dull-face ignorant?
Do you suppose you have a right to a good sight,
    and he or she has no right to a sight?
Do you think matter has cohered together from its diffuse float —
    and the soil is on the surface, and water runs,
    and vegetation sprouts,
For you only, and not for him and her?

19

A man's Body at auction;
I help the auctioneer — the sloven does not half know his business.

20

Gentlemen, look on this wonder!
Whatever the bids of the bidders, they cannot be high enough for it;
For it the globe lay preparing quintillions of years,
    without one animal or plant;
For it the revolving cycles truly and steadily roll'd.

21

In this head the all-baffling brain;
In it and below it, the makings of heroes.

22

Examine these limbs, red, black, or white —
    they are so cunning in tendon and nerve;
They shall be stript, that you may see them.

23

Exquisite senses, life-lit eyes, pluck, volition,
Flakes of breast-muscle, pliant back-bone and neck,
    flesh not flabby, good-sized arms and legs,
And wonders within there yet.

24

Within there runs blood,
The same old blood!
The same red-running blood!
There swells and jets a heart –
    there all passions, desires, reachings, aspirations;
Do you think they are not there because they are not express'd
    in parlours and lecture-rooms?

25

This is not only one man – this is the father of those
    who shall be fathers in their turns;
In him the start of populous states and rich republics;
Of him countless immortal lives, with countless embodiments
    and enjoyments.

26

How do you know who shall come from the offspring of his offspring
    through the centuries?
Who might you find you have come from yourself,
    if you could trace back through the centuries?

A woman's Body at auction!
She too is not only herself – she is the teeming mother of mothers;
She is the bearer of them that shall grow and be mates to the mothers.

Have you ever loved the Body of a woman?
Have you ever loved the Body of a man?
Your father – where is your father?
Your mother – is she living? have you been much with her?
    and has she been much with you?
– Do you not see that these are exactly the same to all,
    in all nations and times, all over the earth?

If any thing is sacred, the human body is sacred,
And the glory and sweet of a man, is the token of manhood untainted;
And in man or woman, a clean, strong, firm-fibred body,
is beautiful as the most beautiful face.

Have you seen the fool that corrupted his own live body?
    or the fool that corrupted her own live body?
For they do not conceal themselves, and cannot conceal themselves.

O my Body! I dare not desert the likes of you in other men and women,
    nor the likes of the parts of you;
I believe the likes of you are to stand or fall with the likes of the Soul,
    (and that they are the Soul;)
I believe the likes of you shall stand or fall with my poems –

and that they are poems,
Man's, woman's, child's, youth's, wife's, husband's,
    mother's, father's, young man's, young woman's poems;
Head, neck, hair, ears, drop and tympan of the ears,
Eyes, eye-fringes, iris of the eye, eye-brows,
    and the waking or sleeping of the lids,
Mouth, tongue, lips, teeth, roof of the mouth,
    jaws and the jaw-hinges,
Nose, nostrils of the nose, and the partition,
Cheeks, temples, forehead, chin, throat,
    back of the neck, neck-slue,
Strong shoulders, manly beard, scapula, hind-shoulders,
    and the ample side-round of the chest.
Upper-arm, arm-pit, elbow-socket, lower-arm,
    arm-sinews, arm-bones,
Wrist and wrist-joints, hand, palm, knuckles, thumb, fore-finger,
    finger-balls, finger-joints, finger-nails,
Broad breast-front, curling hair of the breast, breast-bone, breast-side,
Ribs, belly, back-bone, joints of the back-bone,
Hips, hip-sockets, hip-strength, inward and outward round,
    man-balls, man-root,
Strong set of thighs, well carrying the trunk above,
Leg-fibres, knee, knee-pan, upper-leg, under leg,
Ankles, instep, foot-ball, toes, toe-joints, the heel;
All attitudes, all the shapeliness, all the belongings
    of my or your body, or of any one's body, male or female,
The lung-sponges, the stomach-sac, the bowels sweet and clean,
The brain in its folds inside the skull-frame,
Sympathies, heart-valves, palate-valves, sexuality, maternity,
Womanhood, and all that is a woman –
    and the man that comes from woman,
The womb, the teats, nipples, breast-milk, tears, laughter, weeping,
    love-looks, love-perturbations and risings,
The voice, articulation, language, whispering, shouting aloud,
Food, drink, pulse, digestion, sweat, sleep, walking, swimming,
Poise on the hips, leaping, reclining, embracing,

arm-curving and tightening,
The continual changes of the flex of the mouth, and around the eyes,
The skin, the sun-burnt shade, freckles, hair,
The curious sympathy one feels, when feeling with the hand
    the naked meat of the body,
The circling rivers, the breath, and breathing it in and out,
The beauty of the waist, and thence of the hips,
    and thence downward toward the knees,
The thin red jellies within you, or within me –
    the bones, and the marrow in the bones,
The exquisite realization of health;
O I say, these are not the parts and poems of the Body only,
    but of the Soul,
O I say now these are the Soul!

Walt Whitman

Chosen by **Steven Berkoff**, actor: 'This poem celebrates the simplicity and innocence of humankind in all its physical glory and in its endeavours. It also gives us an insight into the wonders of our own humanity and makes us freshly aware of the miracle of life itself. It shows Whitman as a man of soul and compassion.'

THE GODS OF THE COPYBOOK HEADINGS

As I pass through my incarnations in every age and race,
I make my proper prostrations to the Gods of the Market-
Place.
Peering through reverent fingers I watch them flourish and
fall,
And the Gods of the Copybook Headings, I notice, outlast
them all.

We were living in trees when they met us. They showed us
each in turn
That Water would certainly wet us, as Fire would certainly
burn:
But we found them lacking in Uplift, Vision and Breadth of
Mind,
So we left them to teach the Gorillas while we followed the
March of Mankind.

We moved as the Spirit listed. They never altered their pace,
Being neither cloud nor wind-borne like the Gods of the
Market-Place;
But they always caught up with our progress, and presently
word would come
That a tribe had been wiped off its icefield, or the lights had
gone out in Rome.

With the Hopes that our World is built on they were utterly
out of touch.
They denied that the moon was Stilton; they denied she was
even Dutch.
They denied that Wishes were Horses; they denied that a
Pig had Wings.
So we worshipped the Gods of the Market Who promised
these beautiful things.

When the Cambrian measures were forming, They promised
 perpetual peace.
They swore, if we gave them our weapons, that the wars of
 the tribes would cease.
But when we disarmed They sold us and delivered us bound
 to our foe,
And the Gods of the Copybook Headings said: '*Stick to the
 Devil you know.*'

On the first Feminian Sandstones we were promised the
 Fuller Life
(Which started by loving our neighbour and ended by loving
 his wife)
Till our women had no more children and the men lost
 reason and faith,
And the Gods of the Copybook Headings said: '*The Wages
 of Sin is Death.*'

In the Carboniferous Epoch we were promised abundance
 for all,
By robbing selected Peter to pay for collective Paul;
But, though we had plenty of money, there was nothing our
 money could buy,
And the Gods of the Copybook Headings said: '*If you don't
 work you die.*'

Then the Gods of the Market tumbled, and their smooth-
 tongued wizards withdrew,
And the hearts of the meanest were humbled and began to
 believe it was true.
That All is not Gold that Glitters, and Two and Two make
 Four –
And the Gods of the Copybook Headings limped up to
 explain it once more.

As it will be in the future, it was at the birth of Man –
There are only four things certain since Social Progress
    began:
That the Dog returns to his Vomit and the Sow returns to
    her Mire,
And the burnt Fool's bandaged finger goes wabbling back
    to the Fire;
And that after this is accomplished, and the brave new world
    begins,
When all men are paid for existing and no man must pay for
    his sins,
As surely as Water will wet us, as surely as Fire will burn,
The Gods of the Copybook Headings with terror and
    slaughter return!

Rudyard Kipling

Chosen by **Adrian Berry**, journalist and author: 'Why is this poem meaningful to me? Because it shows the futility and danger of political schemes and social experiments.'

THE HEART SUTRA

Form is emptiness
emptiness is form.
Emptiness is none other than form
form is none other than emptiness.
Likewise feeling, perception, formation,
    and consciousness are emptiness.
All things, Shariputra, are emptiness.
There are no characteristics.
There is no birth and no annihilation.
There is no purity and no impurity.
There is no increase and no decrease.
In emptiness, Shariputra, there is no form,
no feeling, no perception, no formation, no consciousness
no eye, no ear, no nose, no tongue, no body, no mind
no appearance, no sound, no smell, no taste, no touch,
no object of mind
no *dhatu*[6] from the eyes to the mind,
no ignorance, no knowledge
no old age and death,
nor the opposite of old age and death;
no suffering, no beginning of suffering, no end of suffering,
no path, no wisdom, no attainment, and no non-attainment.
Since the *bodhisattvas*[7] have no attainment, Shariputra
they dwell by means of *prajnaparamita*.[8]
Since there are no obstacles of mind, there is no fear.
They go beyond falsehood and reach the finality of nirvana.

---

[6] There are 18 *dhatu* or elements of existence, of which 6 are senses, 6 are qualities,
and 6 are types of consciousness.

[7] *bodhisattva* = a follower of Buddha who has reached the point of illumination short
of nirvana.

[8] *prajnaparamita* = literally 'wisdom-perfection', the collection of Buddhist
scriptures.

All the buddhas of the past, present and future,
by means of *prajnaparamita,*
fully awaken to peerless, perfect enlightenment.
Therefore, the great mantra of *prajnaparamita,*
the mantra of great wisdom,
the highest mantra,
the peerless mantra,
the mantra that calms all suffering,
should be known as truth
(since there is no falsehood).
The *prajnaparamita* mantra is said like this:
OM GATE GATE PARAGATE PARASAM GATE BODHISVAHA
Gone, gone, gone beyond, gone completely beyond.
O, what an awakening!

Attributed to Gautama Buddha (this version by Nigel Watts)

Chosen by **Bernardo Bertolucci**, film director: '"Form is emptiness, emptiness is form." What does this mean? Perhaps by the time I understand it, I won't need to understand it. The emotion is what matters. Not everyone can understand rationally, but almost everyone can understand through their emotions.'

ONE MORE STEP ALONG THE WORLD I GO

One more step along the world I go,
One more step along the world I go.
From the old things to the new,
Keep me travelling along with you.
    And it's from the old I travel to the new.
    Keep me travelling along with you.

Round the corners of the world I turn,
More and more about the world I learn.
All the new things that I see
You'll be looking at along with me.
    And it's from the old I travel to the new.
    Keep me travelling along with you.

As I travel through the bad and good
Keep me travelling the way I should.
Where I see no way to go
You'll be telling me the way, I know.
    And it's from the old I travel to the new.
    Keep me travelling along with you.

Give me courage when the world is rough,
Keep me loving though the world is tough.
Leap and sing in all I do,
Keep me travelling along with you.
    And it's from the old I travel to the new.
    Keep me travelling along with you.

You are older than the world can be,
You are younger than the life in me.
Ever old and ever new,
Keep me travelling along with you.
> *And it's from the old I travel to the new.*
> *Keep me travelling along with you.*

Sydney Carter

Chosen by **Lionel Blue**, rabbi, writer, broadcaster, lecturer and cook: 'I sing this as I go to work in the morning on the London underground. It describes what happens and how I feel.'

Existence is beyond the power of words
To define:
Terms may be used
But none of them absolute.
In the beginning of heaven and earth there were no words,
Words came out of the womb of matter;
And whether a man dispassionately
Sees to the core of life
Or passionately
Sees the surface,
The core and the surface
Are essentially the same,
Words making them seem different
Only to express appearance.
If a name be needed,
Wonder names them both:
From wonder into wonder
Existence opens.

Lao Tzu
(this excerpt from 'The Way of Life' translated
from the Chinese by Witter Bynner)

Chosen by **Dr Leo F. Buscaglia PhD**, author and lecturer: 'It seems to me that the key to a life lived in joy and love lies in embracing that wonder, that mystery, which words will never be able to define. Fortunate is that person who seeks no answers, but rather, embraces that wonder – for he or she will surely find that, in so doing, "From wonder into wonder, existence opens."'

PLANTING A SEQUOIA

All afternoon my brothers and I have worked in the orchard,
Digging this hole, laying you into it, carefully packing the soil.
Rain blackened the horizon, but cold winds kept it over the Pacific,
And the sky above us stayed the dull grey
Of an old year coming to an end.

In Sicily a father plants a tree to celebrate his first son's birth –
An olive or a fig tree – a sign that the earth has one more life to bear.
I would have done the same, proudly laying new stock
     into my father's orchard,
A green sapling rising among the twisted apple boughs,
A promise of new fruit in other autumns.

But today we kneel in the cold planting you, our native giant,
Defying the practical custom of our fathers,
Wrapping in your roots a lock of hair, a piece of an infant's birth cord,
All that remains above earth of a first-born son,
A few stray atoms brought back to the elements.

We will give you what we can – our labour and our soil,
Water drawn from the earth when the skies fail,
Nights scented with the ocean fog, days softened
     by the circuit of bees.
We plant you in the corner of the grove, bathed in western light,
A slender shoot against the sunset.

And when our family is no more, all of his unborn brothers dead,
Every niece and nephew scattered, the house torn down,
His mother's beauty ashes in the air,
I want you to stand among strangers, all young and ephemeral to you,
Silently keeping the secret of your birth.

Dana Gioia

Chosen by **Charles Causley**, writer: 'This poem, arising from the death in infancy of the poet's son Michael Jasper Gioia, is to me as memorable and uplifting both as an elegy and a celebration as anything I have read in the English language.'

UPON A GLOOMY NIGHT

Songs of a joyous soul having arrived
at the height of perfection, union with God
by the path of spiritual negation

On a dark and gloomy night,
With all my loving feelings aroused,
(O venture of joy!)
Without a soul in sight
I left my silent house

Safe and in disguise,
Up the secret stair I climbed,
(O venture of joy!)
Unseen by other eyes
While my house in silence slept

Upon that joyous night
Hidden, invisible to others
Without the need for sight
And with no other guide
Than the burning in my heart

It shone and guided me
More brilliant than a midday sun
To where he waited near
A presence I knew well
At a place no others may appear

Oh night that guided me
Darkness more welcome than dawn's light
Oh night that joined together
The lover and beloved
Uniting them, one unto the other

Inside my ardent breast
Which for him alone I keep entire
He remained deep at rest
And all myself I gifted
Calmed by the cedar-scented breeze

While the early morning winds
Caressed his mane with light breaths,
With his peaceful hand
He wounded my neck and
Numbed my senses with his touch

Forgotten I remained
My face upon my lover rested
All my efforts ceasing
All my cares cast aside
Left among the lilies, abandoned.

St John of the Cross
(translated from the Spanish by John Walden)

Chosen by **Nick Cave**, singer-songwriter and author: ' "Upon a gloomy night"
is not only my most loved spiritual poem, but perhaps also, my favourite love
poem. John speaks of his arrival "at the height of perfection" in terms of
human love at once divine and erotic, where his words seem near incapable of
containing his spiritual rapture.'

PRAYER

Prayer, the Church's banquet, Angels' age,
    God's breath in man returning to his birth,
    The soul in paraphrase, heart in pilgrimage,
The Christian plummet sounding heaven and earth;
Engine against the Almighty, sinner's tower,
    Reversed thunder, Christ-side-piercing spear,
    The six-days' world transposing in an hour,
A kind of tune, which all things hear and fear;
Softness, and peace, and joy, and love, and bliss,
    Exalted manna, gladness of the best,
    Heaven in ordinary, man well drest,
The milky way, the bird of Paradise,
    Church-bells beyond the stars heard, the soul's blood,
    The land of spices; something understood.

George Herbert

Chosen by the **Rt Revd and Rt Hon. Richard Chartres**, Bishop of London: 'Herbert's sonnet articulates the conversation of a person's being with God with a freshness of perception that rises above the ages. To discover "Heaven in ordinary" is our true calling.'

THE TYGER

Tyger! Tyger! burning bright
In the forests of the night,
What immortal hand or eye
Could frame thy fearful symmetry?

In what distant deeps or skies
Burnt the fire of thine eyes?
On what wings dare he aspire?
What the hand dare seize the fire?

And what shoulder, & what art,
Could twist the sinews of thy heart?
And when thy heart began to beat,
What dread hand? & what dread feet?

What the hammer? what the chain?
In what furnace was thy brain?
What the anvil? what dread grasp
Dare its deadly terrors clasp?

When the stars threw down their spears,
And water'd heaven with their tears,
Did he smile his work to see?
Did he who made the Lamb make thee?

Tyger! Tyger! burning bright
In the forests of the night,
What immortal hand or eye
Dare frame thy fearful symmetry?

William Blake

Chosen by **Sri Chinmoy**, student of peace: 'Blake's immortal poem "The Tyger" is humanity's invaluable treasure. Here we see that ignorance-energy, which threatens to devour the whole world, finally discovers its transformation-salvation in the realization of the absolute One. The absolute One embodies both ignorance-energy and knowledge-energy and, at the same time, far transcends them both.'

I THANK YOU GOD FOR MOST THIS AMAZING DAY

i thank You God for most this amazing
day: for the leaping greenly spirits of trees
and a blue true dream of sky; and for everything
which is natural which is infinite which is yes

(i who have died am alive again today,
and this is the sun's birthday; this is the birth
day of life and of love and wings: and of the gay
great happening illimitably earth)

how should tasting touching hearing seeing
breathing any – lifted from the no
of all nothing – human merely being
doubt unimaginable You?

(now the ears of my ears awake and
now the eyes of my eyes are opened)

E. E. Cummings

Chosen by **Sahera Chohan**, broadcaster: 'This poem reminds me of the value of being in the present. It is only when I remember how "amazing" each moment is, that I can share in E. E. Cummings' sense of gratitude.'

OZYMANDIAS

I met a traveller from an antique land
Who said: Two vast and trunkless legs of stone
Stand in the desert. Near them, on the sand,
Half sunk, a shattered visage lies, whose frown,
And wrinkled lip, and sneer of cold command,
Tell that its sculptor well those passions read
Which yet survive, stamped on these lifeless things,
The hand that mocked them, and the heart that fed:
And on the pedestal these words appear:
'My name is Ozymandias, king of kings:
Look on my works, ye Mighty, and despair!'
Nothing beside remains. Round the decay
Of that colossal wreck, boundless and bare
The lone and level sands stretch far away.

Percy Bysshe Shelley

Chosen by the **Rt Hon. Alan Clark MP**: 'This poem is meaningful to me because it is about the transience of authority and worldly power.'

THE APPEAL

If I have given you delight
    By aught that I have done,
Let me lie quiet in that night
    Which shall be yours anon:

And for the little, little span
    The dead are borne in mind,
Seek not to question other than
    The books I leave behind.

Rudyard Kipling

Chosen by **Arthur C. Clarke**, author.

ITHACA

When you start on your journey to Ithaca,
then pray that the road is long,
full of adventure, full of knowledge.
Do not fear the Lestrygonians
and the Cyclopes and the angry Poseidon.
You will never meet such as these on your path,
if your thoughts remain lofty, if a fine
emotion touches your body and your spirit.
You will never meet the Lestrygonians,
the Cyclopes and the fierce Poseidon,
if you do not carry them within your soul,
if your soul does not raise them up before you.

Then pray that the road is long.
That the summer mornings are many,
that you will enter ports seen for the first time
with such pleasure, with such joy!
Stop at Phoenician markets,
and purchase fine merchandise,
mother-of-pearl and corals, amber and ebony,
and pleasurable perfumes of all kinds,
buy as many pleasurable perfumes as you can;
visit hosts of Egyptian cities,
to learn and learn from those who have knowledge.

Always keep Ithaca fixed in your mind.
To arrive there is your ultimate goal.
But do not hurry the voyage at all.
It is better to let it last for long years;
and even to anchor at the isle when you are old,
rich with all that you have gained on the way,
not expecting that Ithaca will offer you riches.

Ithaca has given you the beautiful voyage.
Without her you would never have taken the road.
But she has nothing more to give you.

And if you find her poor, Ithaca has not defrauded you.
With the great wisdom you have gained, with so much experience,
you must surely have understood by then what Ithacas mean.

C. F. Cavafy
(translated from the Greek by Rae Dalven)

Chosen by **Paulo Coelho**, writer.

Also chosen by **Dina Glouberman PhD**, psychotherapist and author: 'This poem is a wonderful antidote to that painful over-emphasis on reaching our ideals that keeps so many of us feeling that if we don't manage to get to a permanently enlightened state filled with love, light and inner peace, then we've got it wrong. This poem somehow offers hope and a real sense of self-worth. We don't need to feel bad that we're still struggling – the journey itself is the source of our pleasure and our creativity, and let it be as long as possible. Ithaca is just a good reason to go on it. Cavafy has some stark lines about actually reaching the ultimate goal. I don't know whether I want to go that far ... I do still cherish some hope that Ithaca will be pretty good.'

Also chosen by the **Rt Hon. Chris Patten**, former Governor of Hong Kong: ' "Ithaca" is full of wise advice about life. It helps, I think, to provide one with some spiritual comfort and balance. I think C. F. Cavafy is one of the wisest of poets; he is particularly good on public affairs and their challenge to private people.'

FROM SLEEP OF PRISONERS

The human heart can go to the lengths of God.
Dark and cold we may be, but this
Is no winter now. The frozen misery
Of centuries breaks, cracks, begins to move;
The thunder is the thunder of the floes,
The thaw, the flood, the upstart Spring.
Thank God our time is now when wrong
Comes up to face us everywhere,
Never to leave us till we take
The longest stride of soul men ever took.
Affairs are now soul size.
The enterprise
Is exploration into God.
What are you making for? It takes
So many thousand years to wake,
But will you wake for pity's sake?

Christopher Fry

Chosen by **Stephanie Cole**, actress: 'This poem is a battle cry as we approach
the new millennium.'

THE STILLNESS OF THE WORLD BEFORE BACH

There must have been a world before
the Trio Sonata in D, a world before the A minor Partitia,
but what kind of world?
A Europe of vast empty spaces, unresounding,
everywhere unawakened instruments
where the Musical Offering, the Well-Tempered Clavier
never passed across the keys.
Isolated churches
where the soprano line of the Passion
never in helpless love twined round
the gentler movements of the flute,
broad soft landscapes
where nothing breaks the stillness
but old woodcutters' axes,
the healthy barking of strong dogs in winter
and, like a bell, skates biting into fresh ice;
the swallows whirring through summer air,
the shell resounding at the child's ear
and nowhere Bach nowhere Bach
the world in a skater's stillness before Bach.

Lars Gustafsson
(translated from the Swedish by Yvonne L. Sandstroem)

Chosen by **Phil Cousineau**, documentary film maker, adventure tour leader and author: 'This magnificent poem about the mystery of the stillness before, in and during life evokes for me the spiritual life as elegantly defined by the Benedictine monk, Brother David Steindl-Rast: "the conscious quest for ultimate answers". One can scarcely breathe during the reading of these brief lines, for they evoke the very stillness at the heart of creation, the stillness of the true seeker, the stillness of Bach himself as he awakened to hear the music of the spheres.'

FROM BODHICHARYAVATARA

As long as space remains,
And as long as sentient beings remain,
May I too remain till that time
To dispel the sufferings of sentient beings.

Shantideva

Chosen by **His Holiness the Dalai Lama.**

Editor's note: This prayer is taken from the chapter on 'Dedication' in the book *Bodhicharyavatara* by the great Buddhist saint-scholar, Shantideva. These four lines represent the essence of the *bodhisattva* ideal of Mahayana Buddhism – that is, the promise which enlightened beings make that they will delay their personal liberation until all other sentient beings are free, a promise known as the '*bodhisattva* vow'.

FROM HAMLET

There's a special providence in the fall of a sparrow.
If it be now, 'tis not to come; if it be not to
come, it will be now; if it be not now, yet it
will come: the readiness is all.

William Shakespeare
(Hamlet, *Act V, Scene II, lines 230–4)*

Chosen by **Dame Judi Dench**, actress.

FROM CYMBELINE

Fear no more the heat o' the sun,
   Nor the furious winter's rages;
Thou thy worldly task hast done,
   Home art gone, and ta'en thy wages:
Golden lads and girls all must,
As chimney-sweepers, come to dust.

Fear no more the frown o' the great;
   Thou art past the tyrant's stroke;
Care no more to clothe and eat;
   To thee the reed is as the oak:
The sceptre, learning, physic, must
All follow this, and come to dust.

Fear no more the lightning flash,
   Nor the all-dreaded thunder-stone;
Fear not slander, censure rash;
   Thou hast finish'd joy and moan:
All lovers young, all lovers must
Consign to thee, and come to dust.

No exorciser harm thee!
Nor no witchcraft charm thee!
Ghost unlaid forbear thee!
Nothing ill come near thee!
Quiet consummation have;
And renowned be thy grave!

William Shakespeare
(Cymbeline, Act IV, Scene II, lines 258–81)

Chosen by **Jonathan Dimbleby**, writer and broadcaster: 'I read this at the memorial service for a dear friend whom I admired. It is optimistic, forgiving, and blessed with peace. It is filled with hope for those who live on, if only they recognize the absence of eternity on earth. It is tender in death.'

THE VISIT AND THE GIFT

At dawn, the moon,
like a creature of fantasy,
stole into my room
and woke me from some
lazy and unproductive sleep.
Her face quickly illuminated
the underside of my soul
and my own being stood
revealed in the naked light.
Sighing in wonder, I
faced my Self, which said:
'Your life so far has chased
the illusion of control:
you will not meet me on that path.
One flash of my glance
is worth a thousand years of piety.'

Overcome by waste and loss,
my soul endarkened itself with shame.
But my moon-faced Self,
whose radiance equalled the sun,
filled a cup of Direct Experience
and urged me to drown my despair:
'No bouquet ... no flavour ...
but this wine can wash away
your being's whole historical library.'

I finished the cup in one gulp,
and, intoxicated by its purity,
fell to the earth.
Since then I am not sure
whether I am here or not.
Neither sober nor drunk,
sometimes I feel the joy of

my soul's eyes looking through mine.
Other times I feel the curl of its hair
and my life bobs and weaves.
Sometimes, from sheer habit,
I'm back on the compost heap.
And sometimes,
when that glance finds me again,
I am back in the Rose Garden.

Sheik Mahmud Shabistari
(version by Neil Douglas-Klotz)

Chosen by **Dr Neil Douglas-Klotz**, independent scholar, translator, author and senior teacher in the Sufi Movement International and the Sufi Islamia Ruhaniat Society: 'This poem expresses those moments in life when, confronted by a vision of the soul, or true self, I am asked to evaluate my life and its preoccupations with control. As I face my inner self, then I need to embrace it all, the honoured and the dishonoured parts. God, so to speak, then becomes more of a reality experienced in everyday life, and that greater Reality leads me towards my next steps. The poem, being 600 years old, also plays with very ecological imagery pointing towards the hidden teacher in one's own "nature".'

WHEN THINGS GO WRONG
AS THEY SOMETIMES WILL

When things go wrong as they sometimes will,
When the road you're trudging seems all uphill,
When the funds are low and the debts are high,
And you want to smile, but you have to sigh.

When care is pressing you down a bit,
Rest if you must, but don't you quit.
Life is queer with its twists and turns,
As every one of us sometimes learns,
And many a failure turns about
When he might have won had he stuck it out.
Don't give up though the pace seems slow –
You may succeed with another blow!

Success is failure turned inside out –
The silver tint of the clouds of doubt,
And you never can tell just how close you are,
It may be near when it seems so far.

So stick to the fight when you're hardest hit –
It's when things seem worst that you must not quit.

Anonymous

Chosen by the **Most Revd Dr Robin Eames**, Archbishop of Armagh, Anglican Primate of All Ireland: 'This poem emphasizes so much of my personal experience in my work for reconciliation in the divisions of Ireland. One moment encouragement, the next frustration – yet the constant vision of a more just and peaceful future for all peoples.'

CARMEN PASCHALE

Last night did Christ the Sun rise from the dark,
The mystic harvest of the fields of God.
    And now the little wandering tribes of bees
    Are brawling in the scarlet flowers abroad.
The winds are soft with birdsong: all night long
    Darkling the nightingale her descant told.
And now inside church doors the happy folk
    The Alleluia chant a hundredfold.
O father of thy flock, be thine by right
    The Easter joy, the threshold of the light.

Sedulius Scottus (AD 848–74)

Chosen by **Dame Paula Fairlie OSB**, Benedictine abbess: 'This poem contains all the freshness and beauty of the first Easter Morning in a Mediterranean land, when nature and humanity are united in acclaiming the Risen Son.'

NIGHT SKY

There came such clear opening of the night sky,
The deep glass of wonders, the dark mind
In unclouded gaze of the abyss
Opened like the expression of a face.
I looked into that clarity where all things are
End and beginning, and saw
My destiny there: 'So,' I said, 'no other
Was possible ever. This
Is I. The pattern stands so for ever.'

What am I? Bound and bounded,
A pattern among the stars, a point in motion
Tracing my way. I am my way: it is I
I travel among the wonders.
Held in that gaze and known
In the eye of the abyss,
'Let it be so,' I said,
And my heart laughed with joy
To know the death I must die.

Kathleen Raine

Chosen by **Reshad Feild**, author: 'This poem was given to me when I first met up with the wonderful "command" in the Tradition of the Sufis – "Die before you die." To die to all the fears that make up the egg-shell of the little "I", so that only the greater "I am" remains. What joy! What unbelievable glory!'

IN A COUNTRY CHURCH

To one kneeling down no word came,
Only the wind's song, saddening the lips
Of the grave saints, rigid in glass;
Or the dry whisper of unseen wings,
Bats not angels, in the high roof.

Was he balked by silence? He kneeled long,
And saw love in a dark crown
Of thorns blazing, and a winter tree
Golden with fruit of a man's body.

R. S. Thomas

Chosen by **Frank Field MP**: 'Thomas expresses better than I can the uncertainties of faith. In his poem "Balance" he writes about "abandon(ing) my theories/ the easier certainties of belief. There are no handrails to grasp."'

Over the ball of it,
    Peering and prying,
How I see all of it,
    Life there, outlying!
Roughness and smoothness,
    Shine and defilement,
Grace and uncouthness:
    One reconcilement.

Orbed as appointed,
    Sister with brother
Joins, ne'er disjointed
    One from the other.
All's lend-and-borrow;
    Good, see, wants evil,
Joy demands sorrow,
    Angel weds devil!

'Which things must – *why* be?'
    Vain our endeavour!
So shall things aye be
    As they were ever.
'Such things should *so* be!'
    Sage our desistence!
Rough-smooth let globe be,
    Mixed – man's existence!

Man – wise and foolish,
   Lover and scorner,
Docile and mulish –
   Keep each his corner!
Honey yet gall of it!
   There's the life lying,
And I see all of it,
   Only, I'm dying!

Robert Browning

Chosen by **Anne Fine**, novelist: 'I think what I like most about this poem is its rattlingly cheerful acceptance of the unreconcilable aspects of life.'

THE OXEN

Christmas Eve, and twelve of the clock.
    'Now they are all on their knees,'
An elder said as we sat in a flock
    By the embers of hearthside ease.

We pictured the meek mild creatures where
    They dwelt in their strawy pen,
Nor did it occur to one of us there
    To doubt they were kneeling then.

So fair a fancy few would weave
    In these years! Yet, I feel,
If someone said on Christmas Eve,
    'Come; see the oxen kneel

'In the lonely barton by yonder coomb
    Our childhood used to know,'
I should go with him in the gloom,
    Hoping it might be so.

Thomas Hardy

Chosen by **Penelope Fitzgerald**, writer: '"Hoping it might be so" means "hoping that I could believe as I did when I was a child", and that is what I hope for.'

THE DARKLING THRUSH

I leant upon a coppice gate
    When Frost was spectre-gray,
And Winter's dregs made desolate
    The weakening eye of day.
The tangled bine-stems scored the sky
    Like strings of broken lyres,
And all mankind that haunted nigh
    Had sought their household fires.

The land's sharp features seemed to be
    The Century's corpse outleant,
His crypt the cloudy canopy,
    The wind his death-lament.
The ancient pulse of germ and birth
    Was shrunken hard and dry,
And every spirit upon earth
    Seemed fervourless as I.

At once a voice arose among
    The bleak twigs overhead
In a full-hearted evensong
    Of joy illimited;
An aged thrush, frail, gaunt, and small,
    In blast-beruffled plume,
Had chosen thus to fling his soul
    Upon the growing gloom.

So little cause for carollings
　　Of such ecstatic sound
Was written on terrestrial things
　　Afar or nigh around,
That I could think there trembled through
　　His happy good-night air
Some blessed Hope, whereof he knew
　　And I was unaware.

Thomas Hardy

Chosen by **Edward Fox**, actor: 'This poem is the observation and perception of a countryman alone, pondering upon the mystery of life and human existence, bravely and with love.'

THE COLLAR

I struck the board, and cried, No more.
I will abroad.
What? shall I ever sigh and pine?
My lines and life are free; free as the road,
Loose as the wind, as large as store.
Shall I be still in suit?
Have I no harvest but a thorn
To let me blood, and not restore
What I have lost with cordial fruit?
Sure there was wine
Before my sighs did dry it: there was corn
Before my tears did drown it.
Is the year only lost to me?
Have I no bays to crown it?
No flowers, no garlands gay? all blasted?
All wasted?
Not so, my heart: but there is fruit,
And thou hast hands.
Recover all thy sigh-blown age
On double pleasures: leave thy cold dispute
Of what is fit, and not. Forsake thy cage,
Thy rope of sands,
Which petty thoughts have made, and made to thee
Good cable, to enforce and draw,
And be thy law,
While thou didst wink and wouldst not see.
Away; take heed:
I will abroad.
Call in thy death's head there: tie up thy fears.
He that forbears
To suit and serve his need,
Deserves his load.
But as I raved and grew more fierce and wild
At every word,

Me thought I heard one calling, *Child !*
And I replied, *My Lord.*

George Herbert

Chosen by **Stephen Fry**, actor and writer: 'This poem perfectly illustrates that those who mock the Church of England should realize that faith has always been a matter of pain and struggle.'

THE WINDHOVER

To Christ our Lord

I caught this morning morning's minion, king-
   dom of daylight's dauphin, dapple-dawn-drawn Falcon, in his
      riding
  Of the rolling level underneath him steady air, and striding
High there, how he rung upon the rein of a wimpling wing
In his ecstasy! then off, off forth on swing,
   As a skate's heel sweeps smooth on a bow-bend: the hurl and
      gliding
   Rebuffed the big wind. My heart in hiding
Stirred for a bird, – the achieve of, the mastery of the thing!

Brute beauty and valour and act, oh, air, pride, plume, here
   Buckle! AND the fire that breaks from thee then, a billion
Times told lovelier, more dangerous, O my chevalier!

   No wonder of it: shéer plód makes plough down sillion
Shine, and blue-bleak embers, ah my dear,
   Fall, gall themselves, and gash gold-vermilion.

Gerard Manley Hopkins

Chosen by **Fiona Fullerton**, actress and writer: 'This poem is hugely enhanced by reading it aloud. It is meant to be spoken, not read in silent contemplation. The reading of it allows one's often troubled spirit to soar in flight with the joyous bird, in all its freedom.'

AN IRISH BLESSING

May the road rise to meet you.
May the wind be always at your back.
May the sun shine warm upon your face,
The rains fall soft upon your fields,
And until we meet again
May God hold you in the palm of his hand.

Anonymous

Chosen by **Sandy Gall CBE**, writer and broadcaster: 'This poem is extremely beautiful, and extremely simple; and it makes me think of a great friend, Andy Skrzypkowiak, killed in the war in Afghanistan, to whom it seems completely appropriate.'

ICE MELTS MY FIRE

I love you, I cry
through the spiralling
wheel web of time.
I love you, I sigh
as the petals
burn up my mind.

'Empty is full,'
she whispers back
through a crack
in time and space.
She's my fiery silver queen,
carrying diamond sutras in her palm
which she pawns
on a juncture
of a dimensional interface,
sending the dharmic wheel
spinning
through inner space.

And the manifestor, set director,
High Inspector,
from the kingdom of souls,
sends an equaliser
in fertiliser,
nourishing the sprouts
of the budding seeds,
that are singing
diamond sutra harmonies,
in faithful bliss of unknowing,
yet thanking God all the same.

And the pawns
in the game
are cashed, checkered,
and spun
through myriad mazes
that we've all begun to see.
Yet the diamond queen's familiar,
from other missions of mercy,
on a galactic harvest
and salvage crew.
As the omniversal mind
plays
polarity duality
with a checkered demon
and a crystal Christ
on a multi-dimensional
Go board of light.

And the diamond sutras
are singing our name
as they dancing emerge into sight
and another strung out soul
is beaded on Buddha's necklace
harmonising a crystal spiral of light.

So sing sweetly
my love,
my earthen vessel
of light.
Your cosmic being
is intergalactically harmonised
and fertilised
by the stars tonight.

As the glass bead game
is sung
in a magic circle
on the edge of the dawn
on the rim of the crystal
sparkling with life.

Eli Jaxon-Bear

Chosen by **Gangaji (Antoinette Varner)**, spiritual teacher: 'Every time I read or hear this poem I experience it more deeply, more fully. Eli, my husband, says he wrote it for me – before we met.'

FROM THE TEMPEST

We are such stuff
As dreams are made on, and our little life
Is rounded with a sleep.

William Shakespeare
(The Tempest, Act IV, Scene I, lines 156–8)

Chosen by **Sir John Gielgud**, actor.

COLTRANE'S PRAYER: A LOVE SUPREME

Thy love become my malice soft-spoken,
my anger harboured in Thy love,
burn my blood to ache despair
yet daybreak comes. My petrified

heart, a stone of this world, reaches
down anew, rooted in Thy name: this
is not the time of dying. Thy beauty
governs me and naked I walk, formless
and forming all heartache's end.

I summon Thy joy windless and still,
and ruddered with God I multiply
the skies. My prayer voices an
overlasting spring, my prayer echoes
God's will back to God, pulse beyond

my pulse in deepening night. Thy name
in my heart is mirror to a galaxy; be
beauty for an hour, says Thy love.
I am unending fire, says Thy love,
and you who do not sing my name shall
be ashes of silence forever in the wind.

O God, make light my shadow; kindle
my fear with radiant, heavenly shafts,
Thy love, to heal and heal again. The
night is ice, my heart beats, and I
read once more divine inscription
on my soul:

a sacred hymn, Thy blessing in my song,
a sacred hymn, Thy everpresent hand.

James Strecker

Chosen by **Evelyn Glennie OBE**, solo percussionist: 'This poem has such a beautiful musical approach; it transports me along improvisational pathways, into the music world and its misunderstood personalities.'

THE SECOND COMING

Turning and turning in the widening gyre
The falcon cannot hear the falconer;
Things fall apart; the centre cannot hold;
Mere anarchy is loosed upon the world,
The blood-dimmed tide is loosed, and everywhere
The ceremony of innocence is drowned;
The best lack all conviction, while the worst
Are full of passionate intensity.

Surely some revelation is at hand;
Surely the Second Coming is at hand.
The Second Coming! Hardly are those words out
When a vast image out of *Spiritus Mundi*
Troubles my sight; somewhere in sands of the desert
A shape with lion body and the head of a man,
A gaze blank and pitiless as the sun,
Is moving its slow thighs, while all about it
Reel shadows of the indignant desert birds.
The darkness drops again; but now I know
That twenty centuries of stony sleep
Were vexed to nightmare by a rocking cradle,
And what rough beast, its hour come round at last,
Slouches towards Bethlehem to be born?

W. B. Yeats

Chosen by **Dr Liz Greene**, astrologer, Jungian analyst, author and director of
the Centre for Psychological Astrology, London: 'In this extraordinary poem,
written in 1919, Yeats describes with power and eloquence the great astrological
cycle of the changing of the ages from Pisces into Aquarius. His prophetic
vision is neither naive nor flowery, and remains, for me, an ongoing warning
of the inevitable eruption of fear, confusion and chaos in the world as all that
has been denied, suppressed or distorted by the spiritual world-view of the last
2,000 years emerges to transform our perceptions of reality. On the surface it is

a bleak poem, although I do not believe that is its deeper implication. It ends with a question, for which I suspect we will have to find the answer as we blunder along.'

PIED BEAUTY

Glory be to God for dappled things –
    For skies of couple-colour as a brinded cow;
      For rose-moles all in stipple upon trout that swim;
Fresh-firecoal chestnut-falls; finches' wings;
    Landscape plotted and pieced – fold, fallow, and plough;
      And áll trádes, their gear and tackle and trim.

All things counter, original, spare, strange;
    Whatever is fickle, freckled (who knows how?)
      With swift, slow; sweet, sour; adazzle, dim;
He fathers-forth whose beauty is past change:
      Praise him.

Gerard Manley Hopkins

Chosen by the **Rt Hon. John Gummer MP**.

Also chosen by **Thomas Keneally**, author: 'This poem is the most dazzling statement I know of transcendence in ordinary visible phenomena.'

HOW CAN MY LIFE GO ON WITHOUT RESONANCE?

I sail and go deep into water,
I swim against the tide,
I resist the overpowering current;
Seconds, minutes and hours betrayed me.
And numerous, countless, gloomy
And lost days let me down
And so did long and empty distances.

My hope ridiculed me,
My goal moved away from me.
I left my companions,
My family members quarrelled with me,
And my neighbour turned into an enemy of mine.

They consulted one another and said,
'You are acting against your interests.'
They began to whisper,
Backbiting and gossiping,
Forgetting me and having a good time together,
Forgetting me and dancing,
Then they would recover and remember,
Repeat things and tell lies,
And give orders with an air of conceit and arrogance,
    'Bend your head to the storm;
Bow in submission to important people.'

No I shall never bend my head to storms,
No, nor shall I ever bow in submission to important people.
How can I abandon my knowledge and learning?
How can I forget my generosity and tolerance?
How can I deform my radiance?
How can I spoil my perfume?
How can I accept and approve of
Being chewed up and spit
By the current of ignorance, the tide of tartars?

How can my life go on without resonance?
How can I forget my family and country, and my yearning?
How can I accept to be shaped by my enemies
Into a frightened gem,
That sleeps on chests,
Indifferent and immobile?

What do you want?
What do you have in mind?
Do you want me to swim,
To sail with the current?
Do you think I will walk about
Without an identity or number?
Would you be satisfied with my destruction?
Would you be content with my loss?
In the tumult of the sea?
Without any ports or harbours,
To be imprisoned by the chief traitor,
Who would torture me, crush me, reject me,
And then drop me, with great stupidity,
In the desert or on a coast,
Unable to hear or feel,
Without any vision or any life,
And hang on my chest
A medal of cheating and falsehood, or of tin,
And adorn my head with a crown
Of hypocrisy, flattery and frost?

It is true that I do sail
In the seas of despair,
And true that I fight the currents
And the fits of hopelessness,
True that I do swim
In lakes of wretchedness
Against all currents
Of inflexibility and unjust accusations,
Without a weapon and without conditions.
Since my oars were broken,
My companion committed suicide,
And my vessel exploded
Among the storms and afflictions and in the midst of conspiracy,
I resist and fight
And wrestle with the tide and the waves,
And I do not care if I die.

But, I do care to die
Standing up and erect,
Like the milestones and monuments,
As a symbol of obstinacy, challenge,
Opposition and steadfastness,
With faith that God is one.

Hisham Ali Hafiz

Chosen by **Hisham Ali Hafiz**, newspaper proprietor and poet: 'I like this poem because it expresses as forcefully as possible my innermost feelings about various aspects and challenges in life, my aversion to injustice and tyranny, and rejection of submission to anybody except Almighty God.'

FORGIVE ME

Forgive me if I do not cry
The day you die,
Streams at some seasons
Wind their way through country lanes of beauty
And are dry.

The willow bends its head
To kiss the empty river bed
With the same caress it gave
When in its heyday it was full and high
Oh river know that I remember
The splashing laughing clatter
Of a bubbling day in Spring
When everything was blossoming!

Butterflies still hover
Down the rocky bed
And weeds grow strong and
Guard the pebbled way.
In this high noon of nothing
Which is death
Brave flags still wave
Cowslip-parsley, rag weed and sorrel
Shout to me
That Spring is on her way
Comfort, I am still too deaf to hear.

Yet forgive me if I do not cry
The day you die
The simplest reason that I know
You said you'd rather have it so
And that I held my head serenely high
Remembering the love and glory that we knew.
Forgive me if I do not cry

The day you die....
Forgive me
If I do....

Sarah Churchill

Chosen by **Nigel Hawthorne**, actor: 'This poem was written by Sarah Churchill about her father Winston Churchill. Sarah's background as a child was very much in the shadow of her famous and brilliant father. I find similar parallels in my own life, though my family connections were by no means as illustrious. But I too had an awkward relationship with my father – a rather Churchillian-looking man, strong willed, often remote and Victorian in his attitudes. I, too, incurred parental displeasure by breaking with convention and going into the theatre. Sarah's reconciliation with her father is movingly described in her book *A Thread in the Tapestry*, and her memorial poem to him is deeply affecting, as I'm sure you'll agree. Perhaps I envy her that reconciliation, for my own with my father didn't happen, though there was a softening. But, most of all, I admire her hugely emotional response to her father's death. It's a wonderful piece. So simple.'

IT IS AN HONOURABLE THOUGHT

It is an honourable Thought
And makes One lift One's Hat
As One met sudden Gentlefolk
Upon a daily Street
That We've immortal Place
Though Pyramids decay
And Kingdoms, like the Orchard
Flit Russetly away.

Emily Dickinson

Chosen by **Denis Healey (Lord Healey of Riddlesden)**: 'Emily Dickinson could not accept the Church as an institution, nor confine her spiritual experience to Christianity. Yet she, like many others, including myself, believed in the everlasting reality of the spirit, and expressed her feeling with unique simplicity.'

MAN AND THE ECHO

Man
In a cleft that's christened Alt
Under broken stone I halt
At the bottom of a pit
That broad noon never lit,
And shout a secret to the stone.
All that I have said and done,
Now that I am old and ill,
Turns into a question till
I lie awake night after night
And never get the answers right.
Did that play of mine send out
Certain men the English shot?
Did words of mine put too great strain
On that woman's reeling brain?
Could my spoken words have checked
That whereby a house lay wrecked?
And all seems evil until I
Sleepless would lie down and die.

Echo
Lie down and die.

Man
                                    That were to shirk
The spiritual intellect's great work
And shirk it in vain. There is no release
In a bodkin or disease,
Nor can there be a work so great
As that which cleans man's dirty slate.
While man can still his body keep
Wine or love drug him to sleep,
Waking he thanks the Lord that he
Has body and its stupidity,

But body gone he sleeps no more
And till his intellect grows sure
That all's arranged in one clear view
Pursues the thoughts that I pursue,
Then stands in judgement on his soul,
And, all work done, dismisses all
Out of intellect and sight
And sinks at last into the night.

Echo
Into the night.

Man
           O rocky voice
Shall we in that great night rejoice?
What do we know but that we face
One another in this place?
But hush, for I have lost the theme,
Its joy or night seem but a dream;
Up there some hawk or owl has struck
Dropping out of sky or rock,
A stricken rabbit is crying out
And its cry distracts my thought.

W. B. Yeats

Chosen by **Seamus Heaney**, poet: 'This is a poem about a person *in extremis*, driven to consult the oracle, desperate for ultimate truths. But the oracle's response turns out to be an echo, and the poet ends as he began, up against the cliff-face of his own mortality. Nevertheless, the cliff has answered the prayer for enlightenment with a poem which rhymes "voice" with "rejoice", "shirk" with "work", "crying out" with "thought", a poem which thereby insinuates that the human spirit is a vital and resourceful element, capable of outfacing pain and exhaustion, or at the very least, capable of turning them to artistic advantage.'

CHRIST'S LOVE-SONG

Love me brought,
And love me wrought,
   Man, to be thy fere.[9]
Love me fed,
And love me led
   And love me lettet[10] here.

Love me slew,
And love me drew,
   And love me laid on bier.
Love is my peace;
For love I chese,[11]
   an to buyen dear.

Ne dread thee nought,
I have thee sought,
   Bothen day and night,
To haven thee;
Well is me,
   I have thee won in fight.

Anon

---

[9] fere = mate
[10] lettet = allows
[11] chese = chose

and

I SHALL SAY WHAT INORDINATE LOVE IS

I shall say what inordinate love is;
The furiosity and wodness[12] of mind,
An instinguible burning, faulting bliss,
A great hunger, insatiate to find,
A dulcet ill, an evil sweetness blind,
A right wonderful sugared sweet error
Without labour rest, contrary to kind,
Or without quiet, to have huge labour.

Anon (fifteenth century)

Chosen by **John Horder**, poet, storyteller, performer, teacher and journalist: 'I adore the first of these poems as a deeply wonderful and amazing poem and song that demands to be read aloud. It (and particularly the devastating last line, "I have thee won in fight") embodies the combative love/hate relationship I have enjoyed with Meher Baba for the past 30 years or so.

'I must also nominate another poem by Anon, "I Shall Say What Inordinate Love Is". Anon is the most living embodiment of the collective voice of all English, Irish, Welsh, African and Indian ancestors. I adore Anon even more than I do Rumpelstiltskin or Meher Baba.'

---

[12] wodness = frenzy

GLAD DAY

A dawn of agitating winds
dapples leaves afresh on skylit space
awakening alps of cloud to race
& drop out, giving way to sun
as firm in its good morning beams
– A tonic lightening good morrow
crystalling adjective in noun,
name in thing – another day
– another moment in an eternal ray
of running magic rhythm's no-time
releasing madhappy conjunctions
of plenitude – unplanned
realisations
        of being alive –
This is a day, you say
for visions and miracles
and cleansing the sights
– A day I want to wear green
and orange
– No – stay naked, I cry, I sigh
but it makes no odds as
tingling to one another
we leap out of bed as one
man, yes – that's to say
feeling like nothing we knew before,
like – as if nothing *was*
before, like – 'a new man'
– two persons in one
being – animal mental spiritual
poised – in perfect union
of sentient immortality –
    Jump now – let's
out and away, slide down
the stairs Whisht – athwart

sleep's lingering portico – heavy jambs
flung open wide eyes drive on
our twinkle-toed electric glee, dive
on down under the blazing stoop
– toss our heads letting hair stream
wild & free, floating the tree-lined arcade's green-
   gold shimmering budfall blossomdrift
we run run run print our pleasure in
springing foot momentum – touching
down only to whizz on faster
not quite in step but gaily zig-zag hand
in hand, foot evenly over-
lapping foot as if to tip
all conflicts deftly down the drains'
fetid jaws –
   Lifting by treading
this crumbling vale – Notting Dale
– called London's 'Jungle West 11',
discounting clerical steps to heaven
– finding our feet, the day's
and sensing those that did
in ancient time

   ... Comes midday, you're mental miles away –
slowed, tamed, pacing – at bay
feeding hungry underprivileged & immigrant mites
the vegetable university lies of the land
– another mind and matter 'weekday'
where mountains drop back
to the classroom wall –

   I'm back on the balcony, writing –
studying my hand, thinking over
my thirty years – dismantled, spent
– after-knowledge of the good
– miraculous – yes, and the terrible

hours of an age – lashes my spirit,
shackles limbs – to burrow the margin
of memory's heavy page

   – and yet … the earth is full
of sky today, and the ageless ancestral sky
on fire – as they say,
paving the streets
                  with gold
– so arise, awake again
to fresh splendours
of measured possibility
– this super-natural
real world – & the immeasurable beyond!
   Born every day
      – tho' every moment
      the weighed heart
      out
          burst
              its load
– so do flowers – mandalas –
the throbbing universe
our very breath
– all ours – the stars, O love
the only power
        I'll ever crave.

   Too soon – late afternoon
the tide of exultation ebbs away, so –
   I'll walk out to meet you,
   past the glistening panoply
   of plastic & aluminium offices, uptown
   from the sodium-sentinelled glare
   of cheaper, newly faded tower blocks
   looking custom-built for battery, rape or suicide
over the once hallowed ground of play-street trysts

and bombsite chase – the long-lost
yearnings, fears and fleeting triumphs
– humiliation, relief – and still more
grief for my own child city
                    so barely covered over
   – yet the earth is full the twilit air
busy with rumours of day's work done, this day's
   children home – a moving range
of lamby peaks spreading the evening
out against the night, as lights
flash on in ones and twos, the kids
come out again to play
with ball and bow, and tear away
to catch up a piper
   who's chasing the sunset
      round the corner
– dancing, delirious with its promise
of summers galore – glad shouts

   ... their heads go under
swimming through the deep-end dusk –
long-shadowed cascades
                        hours after closing time
   I see them drunk – lose themselves
and their long days' journeys
in the void waves' ripple-responses
– mounting
            and breaking with them
to aeons, where nothing is recognised
– know death
and surface in the nick of time, riding
high – flailing kicking gasping alive

   ... and know
the weariless labour of love
Blake's little black boy's mother knew

we each
    'are put on earth a little space,
    that we may learn to bear'
is the one undying deliverance
– to embrace the burning joy
at the heart of creation – burning
    for continuous renewal
    of life, the only measure
    of its worth –

    O – let all my safety
catches be blown – undone
for I hear voices – singing, calling, avalanching –
murmuring on toward
               distant shores and forests
as we navigate the winds and whirlpools
on our ship of words made flesh – your words
blasting open my ears to the eaves
when you turn from dream to whisper
    – You are the key
    to all my secret doors
    that grew rusty on their hinges
– and I turn
        on
and on
resplendent
    in you
            – and we open
            all the doors
      unto the innermost
      dawning
           vision
– wing'd riders
of apocalypse
      – each night
    and opened day

revealed –
full flight
in the shining armour
of naked light

Michael Horovitz

Chosen by **Michael Horovitz**, poet: 'This poem was written in autumn 1966 for Frances Horovitz (1938–83). We'd met and fallen in love six years previously, and got married in the spring of '66. Frances is the "you" addressed, and spoke the phrases quoted in italics near the beginning and the end. The poem is named after the Blake engraving *Morning* or *Glad Day* of 1780. It is not intended as an explicit gloss on the picture, more as an incidental homage to what I take to be its essence. Edward Lucie-Smith has aptly defined what Blake conveys here as "the soul of man springing forth into the consciousness of his own power". The poem traces a reawakening of wonder and delight, a single glad day of my life.'

Or ever the silver cord be loosed,
Or the golden bowl be broken,
Or the pitcher be broken at the fountain,
Or the wheel broken at the cistern.
Then shall the dust return to the earth as it was:
And the spirit shall return unto God who gave it.

The Holy Bible, Authorized Version

Chosen by **Sir Fred Hoyle FRS**, astronomer and writer: 'Had I been the Prime Minister I would have chosen to read these lines at the funeral of Diana, Princess of Wales. Had I chanced to be Archbishop of Canterbury I would have made the same choice. For in my opinion these are the best lines anywhere in the Bible.'

FROM FACTS OF THE FAITH

Death is nothing at all.
It does not count.
I have only slipped away into the next room.
Nothing has happened.
Everything remains exactly as it was.
I am I, and you are you,
And the old life we lived so fondly together
    is untouched, unchanged.
Whatever we were to each other, that we still are.

Call me by my old familiar name.
Speak to me in the easy way which you always used.
Put no difference in your tone,
Wear no forced air of solemnity or sorrow.
Laugh as we always laughed at the little jokes
    that we enjoyed together.
Play, smile, think of me, pray for me.
Let my name be ever the household word
    that it always was,
let it be spoken without effort, without the trace
    of a shadow on it.

Life means all that it ever meant,
It is the same as it ever was.
There is absolute and unbroken continuity.
What is this death but a negligible accident?
Why should I be out of mind because I am out of sight?

I am waiting for you, for an interval,
somewhere very near, just around the corner.
All is well.
Nothing is hurt; nothing is lost.
One brief moment and all will be as it was before.
How we shall laugh at the trouble of parting
    when we meet again!

Henry Scott Holland

Chosen by **Gloria Hunniford**, TV and radio interviewer: 'This poem was spoken at the memorial service of my former husband, Don Keating, in January 1997. It contains words which were of great comfort – not only to me, but to my children.'

MEDITATION

With an ancient love worn down by pity, anger and solitude

O.V. DE L. MILOSZ

Lord, it is quite possible that people, while praising you, were mistaken.
You were not a ruler on a throne to whom from here below
prayers and the smoke of incense ascend.
The throne they imagined was empty and you smiled bitterly
Seeing that they turn to you with the hope
That you will protect their crops from hail and their bodies from illness,
That you save them from pestilence, hunger, fire and war.
A wanderer, camping by invisible waters, you would keep a
little flame hardly visible in darkness.
And sitting by it, pensive, you would shake your head.
So much you wanted to help them, glad any time you succeeded,
You felt compassion for them, forgiving them their mistake,
Their falsity, of which they were aware, pretending they did not know it,
And even their ugliness, as they gathered in their churches.
Lord, my heart is full of admiration and I want to talk with you,
For I am sure you understand me, in spite of my contradictions.
It seems to me that now I learned at last what it means to love people
And why love is worn down by loneliness, pity, and anger.
It is enough to reflect strongly and persistently on one life,
On a certain woman, for instance, as I am doing now
To perceive the greatness of those – weak – creatures
Who are able to be honest, brave in misfortune, and patient till the end.
What can I do more, Lord, than to meditate on all that
And stand before you in the attitude of an implorer
For the sake of their heroism asking: Admit us to your glory.

Czeslaw Milosz

Chosen by **Dr Michael Ignatieff**, writer.

CAST ALL YOUR VOTES FOR DANCING

I know the voice of depression
Still calls to you.

I know those habits that can ruin your life
Still send their invitations.

But you are with the Friend now
And look so much stronger.

You can stay that way
And even bloom!

Keep squeezing drops of the Sun
From your prayers and work and music
And from your companions' beautiful laughter.

Keep squeezing drops of the Sun
From the sacred hands and glance of your Beloved
And, my dear,
From the most insignificant movements
Of your own holy body.

Learn to recognize the counterfeit coins
That may buy you just a moment of pleasure,
But then drag you for days
Like a broken man
Behind a farting camel.

You are with the Friend now.
Learn what actions of yours delight Him,
What actions of yours bring freedom
And Love.

Whenever you say God's name, dear pilgrim,
My ears wish my head was missing
So they could finally kiss each other
And applaud all your nourishing wisdom!

O keep squeezing drops of the Sun
From your prayers and work and music
And from your companions' beautiful laughter
And from the most insignificant movements
Of your own holy body.

Now, sweet one,
Be wise.
Cast all your votes for Dancing!

Hafiz
(translated by Daniel Ladinsky)

Chosen by **Dr Rosie Jackson**, novelist and non-fiction writer: 'In 1978, when I was lecturing in literature at the University of East Anglia, my life was completely overturned by contact with the Indian master Avatar Meher Baba (1894–1969), who reawoke my love of mysticism and whom I have been following ever since. Amongst the Sufi poets Baba most enjoyed – Rumi, Hafiz and Kabir – it was Hafiz (c. 1320–89, known in Persia as "the tongue of the invisible") who was his favourite for capturing the very essence of the spiritual path. I now read Hafiz time and again for his passion, his clarity, his irreverent humour, his radiant invocations to joy and freedom, and his one-pointed devotion to God – a God made intimate and addressed in human terms as the Beloved, the Friend – the One who mirrors our own divinity. This particular poem – in a wonderful new version by Daniel Ladinsky – is pinned above my desk for inspiration when I write, to remind me of the real priorities. And while its notion of dancing can be taken literally – as with Sufism's "whirling dervishes" – it's as much a metaphor for the ecstasy and intoxication that accompany surrender to divine love.'

DOVER BEACH

The sea is calm to-night.
The tide is full, the moon lies fair
Upon the straits; – on the French coast the light
Gleams and is gone; the cliffs of England stand,
Glimmering and vast, out in the tranquil bay.
Come to the window, sweet is the night-air!
Only, from the long line of spray
Where the sea meets the moon-blanched sand,
Listen! you hear the grating roar
Of pebbles which the waves draw back, and fling,
At their return, up the high strand,
Begin, and cease, and then again begin,
With tremulous cadence slow, and bring
The eternal note of sadness in.
Sophocles long ago
Heard it on the Ægæan, and it brought
Into his mind the turbid ebb and flow
Of human misery; we
Find also in the sound a thought,
Hearing it by this distant northern sea.

The Sea of Faith
Was once, too, at the full, and round earth's shore
Lay like the folds of a bright girdle furl'd.
But now I only hear
Its melancholy, long, withdrawing roar,
Retreating, to the breath
Of the night-wind, down the vast edges drear
And naked shingles of the world.

Ah, love, let us be true
To one another! for the world, which seems
To lie before us like a land of dreams,
So various, so beautiful, so new,

Hath really neither joy, nor love, nor light,
Nor certitude, nor peace, nor help for pain;
And we are here as on a darkling plain
Swept with confused alarms of struggle and flight,
Where ignorant armies clash by night.

Matthew Arnold

Chosen by **William Johnston**, Jesuit Catholic priest, formerly Professor of Religious Studies and Director of the Institute of Oriental Studies at Sophia University, Tokyo: 'This poem is relevant today. It describes poignantly the loss of faith in Matthew Arnold's day. And what is the answer? "Ah, love, let us be true to one another." The answer is deep, faithful human love. Surely this is the answer that will appeal to men and women of the twenty-first century who are searching for a deep, human love that will lead them to God.'

THE SERENITY PRAYER

God grant me
The serenity to accept
The things I cannot change,
Courage
To change the things I can,
And wisdom always
to tell the
difference.

Anonymous

and

LATE FRAGMENT

And did you get what
you wanted from this life, even so?
I did.
And what did you want?
To call myself beloved, to feel myself
beloved on the earth.

Raymond Carver

Chosen by **A. L. Kennedy**, author: 'I first read "The Serenity Prayer" about 15 years ago and – for a variety of reasons – it's come to be close to the centre of what efforts I make to live a life of peace or perspective. It certainly makes it easier to be a human being around other human beings.

'"Late Fragment" represents both a truth and an aspiration. I don't believe I've ever understood God's love, other than through human love. I have yet to feel myself beloved on the earth, but I think there is little else worth the candle in life, other than to love and be loved. It would be the finest epitaph and was, of course, one of Carver's.

'Both suggestions mean a great deal to me.'

LOVE

Love bade me welcome; yet my soul drew back,
    Guilty of dust and sin.
But quick-eyed Love, observing me grow slack
    From my first entrance in,
Drew nearer to me, sweetly questioning,
    If I lacked anything.

'A guest,' I answered, 'worthy to be here.'
    Love said, 'You shall be he.'
'I, the unkind, ungrateful? Ah, my dear,
    I cannot look on thee.'
Love took my hand, and smiling, did reply,
    'Who made the eyes but I?'

'Truth, Lord, but I have marred them: let my shame
    Go where it doth deserve.'
'And know you not,' says Love, 'who bore the blame?'
    'My dear, then I will serve.'
'You must sit down,' says Love, 'and taste my meat.'
    So I did sit and eat.

George Herbert

Chosen by **Sir Ludovic Kennedy**, writer and broadcaster: 'Although I am not a Christian, "Love" has for a long time been my favourite poem. I think the reason is that while the word "love" is in the poem, the alternative word "God" itself never appears and the word "Lord" only once. It is a beautifully structured poem and I seldom read it to myself or aloud without tears.'

Also chosen by **Tim Pigott-Smith**, actor and director: 'In Herbert's mind, of course, the meaning of the poem is specifically religious; but for me it is suffused with the transforming power of Love – love of any kind.'

Also chosen by **Sir Roy Strong**, writer, historian and gardener: 'This poem says everything about God's never-ending forgiveness and love.'

Also chosen by **Emma Thompson**, actress.

PSALM 104

Bless the Lord, my soul!
Lord God, how great you are,
clothed in majesty and glory,
wrapped in light as in a robe!

You stretch out the heavens like a tent.
Above the rains you build your dwelling.
You make the clouds your chariot,
you walk on the wings of the wind,
you make the winds your messengers
and flashing fire your servants.

You founded the earth on its base,
to stand firm from age to age.
You wrapped it with the ocean like a cloak:
the waters stood higher than the mountains.

At your threat they took to flight;
at the voice of your thunder they fled.
They rose over the mountains and flowed down
to the place which you had appointed.
You set limits they might not pass
lest they return to cover the earth.

You make springs gush forth in the valleys:
they flow in between the hills.
They give drink to all the beasts of the field;
the wild-asses quench their thirst.
On the banks dwell the birds of heaven;
from the branches they sing their song.

From your dwelling you water the hills;
earth drinks its fill of your gift.
You make the grass grow for the cattle

and the plants to serve man's needs,
that he may bring forth bread from the earth
and wine, to cheer man's heart;
oil, to make his face shine
and bread to strengthen man's heart.

The trees of the Lord drink their fill,
the cedars he planted on Lebanon;
there the birds build their nests:
on the tree-top the stork has her home.
The goats find a home on the mountains
and rabbits hide in the rocks.

You made the moon to mark the months;
the sun knows the time for its setting.
When you spread the darkness it is night
and all the beasts of the forest creep forth.
The young lions roar for their prey
and ask their food from God.

At the rising of the sun they steal away
and go to rest in their dens.
Man goes forth to his work,
to labour till evening falls.

How many are your works, O Lord!
In wisdom you have made them all.
The earth is full of your riches.

There is the sea, vast and wide,
with its moving swarms past counting,
living things great and small.
The ships are moving there
and the monsters you made to play with.

All of these look to you
to give them their food in due season.
You give it, they gather it up:
you open your hand, they have their fill.

You hide your face, they are dismayed;
you take back your spirit, they die,
returning to the dust from which they came.
You send forth your spirit, they are created;
and you renew the face of the earth.

May the glory of the Lord last for ever.
May the Lord rejoice in his works!
He looks on the earth and it trembles;
the mountains send forth smoke at his touch.

I will sing to the Lord all my life,
make music to my God while I live.
May my thoughts be pleasing to him.
I find my joy in the Lord.
Let sinners vanish from the earth
and the wicked exist no more.

Bless the Lord, my soul.

The Holy Bible

Chosen by **Bruce Kent**, retired priest: 'This is my favourite religious poem. It speaks to me of God, of his care for all of creation, of which we are a part, and of the joy of being part of it all.'

STRANGE MEETING

It seemed that out of battle I escaped
Down some profound dull tunnel, long since scooped
Through granites which titanic wars had groined.

Yet also there encumbered sleepers groaned,
Too fast in thought or death to be bestirred.
Then, as I probed them, one sprang up, and stared
With piteous recognition in fixed eyes,
Lifting distressful hands, as if to bless.
And by his smile, I knew that sullen hall –
By his dead smile I knew we stood in Hell.

With a thousand pains that vision's face was grained;
Yet no blood reached there from the upper ground,
And no guns thumped, or down the flues made moan.
'Strange friend,' I said, 'here is no cause to mourn.'
'None,' said the other, 'save the undone years,
The hopelessness. Whatever hope is yours,
Was my life also; I went hunting wild
After the wildest beauty in the world,
Which lies not calm in eyes, or braided hair,
But mocks the steady running of the hour,
And if it grieves, grieves richlier than here.
For by my glee might many men have laughed,
And of my weeping something had been left,
Which must die now. I mean the truth untold,
The pity of war, the pity war distilled.
Now men will go content with what we spoiled,
Or, discontent, boil bloody, and be spilled.
They will be swift with swiftness of the tigress.
None will break ranks, though nations trek from progress.
Courage was mine, and I had mystery,
Wisdom was mine, and I had mastery:
To miss the march of this retreating world

Into vain citadels that are not walled.
Then, when much blood had clogged their chariot-wheels,
I would go up and wash them from sweet wells,
Even with truths that lie too deep for taint.
I would have poured my spirit without stint
But not through wounds; not on the cess of war.
Foreheads of men have bled where no wounds were.

'I am the enemy you killed, my friend.
I knew you in this dark: for so you frowned
Yesterday through me as you jabbed and killed.
I parried; but my hands were loath and cold.
Let us sleep now....'

Wilfred Owen

Chosen by **Glenys Kinnock**, Labour Member of the European Parliament for South Wales East: 'The poem evokes feelings of horror at the tragedy of the First World War. It is written in Owen's stark truthfulness. He is eloquent about the "pity of war" and about the empathy he felt with the German soldier, who, like him, had in the past experienced joy and happiness, but now had only hopelessness and death. There is a message of understanding and forgiveness and the poem conveys so much in a poignant way about the pointless nature of that war. Owen writes more eloquently than any other poet about the heartache, suffering and loneliness which war brings to the soldier. He never abdicated his own perceived responsibility to share the suffering of others. "Strange Meeting" has stark images of hell – the reality of the Western Front that has lingered on since the first time I read it when I was 16. We face no greater responsibility than the need to ensure that, on our own continent, we never again take up arms against each other. It is also, of course, our responsibility to ensure that all our world's citizens can live in peace and security together. Wars have no winners, and war and poverty are today inseparable.'

To every thing there is a season,
And a time to every purpose under the heaven:
A time to be born, and a time to die;
A time to plant, and a time to pluck up that which is planted;
A time to kill, and a time to heal;
A time to break down, and a time to build up;
A time to weep, and a time to laugh;
A time to mourn, and a time to dance;
A time to cast away stones, and a time to gather stones together;
A time to embrace, and a time to refrain from embracing;
A time to get, and a time to lose;
A time to keep, and a time to cast away;
A time to rend, and a time to sew;
A time to keep silence, and a time to speak;
A time to love, and a time to hate;
A time of war, and a time of peace.

The Holy Bible, Authorized Version

Chosen by the **Rt Hon. Neil Kinnock**, European Commissioner: 'This is a complete poem – beautiful in the way that the very simple language conveys the most profound truths as well as being rhythmic and balanced. Most of all, these verses are rational and peace-giving without being fatalistic: the choice of all "times", other than birth and death, is for human beings to make consciously. Because of that, the poetry is inspirational as well as consoling.'

RETURNING TO THE ROOT

Be completely empty.
Be perfectly serene.
The ten thousand things arise together;
in their arising is their return.
Now they flower,
and flowering
sink homeward,
returning to the root.

The return to the root
is peace.
Peace: to accept what must be,
to know what endures.
In that knowledge is wisdom.
Without it, ruin, disorder.

To know what endures
is to be openhearted,
magnanimous,
regal,
blessed,
following the Tao,
the way that endures forever.
The body comes to its ending,
but there is nothing to fear.

Lao Tzu
(this version by Ursula K. Le Guin)

Chosen by **Ursula K. Le Guin**, writer: 'All my life Lao Tzu's poetry has comforted my soul, for he affirms morality without a deity to confuse it, and a spirituality of which man is not the measure.'

GOD'S GRANDEUR

The world is charged with the grandeur of God.
    It will flame out, like shining from shook foil;
    It gathers to a greatness, like the ooze of oil
Crushed. Why do men then now not reck his rod?
Generations have trod, have trod, have trod;
    And all is seared with trade; bleared, smeared with toil;
    And wears man's smudge and shares man's smell: the soil
Is bare now, nor can foot feel, being shod.

And for all this, nature is never spent;
    There lives the dearest freshness deep down things;
And though the last lights off the black West went
    Oh, morning, at the brown brink eastward, springs –
Because the Holy Ghost over the bent
    World broods with warm breast and with ah! bright wings.

Gerard Manley Hopkins

Chosen by **Doris Lessing**, writer: 'I think this is one of the greatest religious poems ever written.'

Also chosen by **Jonathon Porritt**, environmentalist.

ELEGY WRITTEN IN A COUNTRY CHURCHYARD

The curfew tolls the knell of parting day,
  The lowing herd wind slowly o'er the lea,
The plowman homeward plods his weary way,
  And leaves the world to darkness and to me.

Now fades the glimm'ring landscape on the sight,
  And all the air a solemn stillness holds,
Save where the beetle wheels his droning flight,
  And drowsy tinklings lull the distant folds;

Save that from yonder ivy-mantled tow'r
  The moping owl does to the moon complain
Of such, as wand'ring near her secret bow'r,
  Molest her ancient solitary reign.

Beneath those rugged elms, that yew-tree's shade,
  Where heaves the turf in many a mould'ring heap,
Each in his narrow cell for ever laid,
  The rude forefathers of the hamlet sleep.

The breezy call of incense-breathing Morn,
  The swallow twitt'ring from the straw-built shed,
The cock's shrill clarion, or the echoing horn,
  No more shall rouse them from their lowly bed.

For them no more the blazing hearth shall burn,
  Or busy housewife ply her evening care:
No children run to lisp their sire's return,
  Or climb his knees the envied kiss to share.

Oft did the harvest to their sickle yield,
  Their furrow oft the stubborn glebe has broke;
How jocund did they drive their team afield!
  How bow'd the woods beneath their sturdy stroke!

Let not Ambition mock their useful toil,
    Their homely joys, and destiny obscure;
Nor Grandeur hear with a disdainful smile
    The short and simple annals of the poor.

The boast of heraldry, the pomp of pow'r,
    And all that beauty, all that wealth e'er gave,
Awaits alike th'inevitable hour.
    The paths of glory lead but to the grave.

Nor you, ye proud, impute to these the fault,
    If Mem'ry o'er their tomb no trophies raise,
Where thro' the long-drawn aisle and fretted vault
    The pealing anthem swells the note of praise.

Can storied urn or animated bust
    Back to its mansion call the fleeting breath?
Can Honour's voice provoke the silent dust,
    Or Flatt'ry soothe the dull cold ear of Death?

Perhaps in this neglected spot is laid
    Some heart once pregnant with celestial fire;
Hands, that the rod of empire might have sway'd,
    Or wak'd to ecstasy the living lyre.

But Knowledge to their eyes her ample page
    Rich with the spoils of time did ne'er unroll;
Chill Penury repress'd their noble rage,
    And froze the genial current of the soul.

Full many a gem of purest ray serene,
    The dark unfathom'd caves of ocean bear:
Full many a flow'r is born to blush unseen,
    And waste its sweetness on the desert air.

Some village-Hampden, that with dauntless breast
 The little tyrant of his fields withstood;
Some mute inglorious Milton here may rest,
 Some Cromwell guiltless of his country's blood.

Th'applause of list'ning senates to command,
 The threats of pain and ruin to despise,
To scatter plenty o'er a smiling land,
 And read their hist'ry in a nation's eyes,

Their lot forbade: nor circumscrib'd alone
 Their growing virtues, but their crimes confin'd;
Forbade to wade through slaughter to a throne,
 And shut the gates of mercy on mankind,

The struggling pangs of conscious truth to hide,
 To quench the blushes of ingenious shame,
Or heap the shrine of Luxury and Pride
 With incense kindled at the Muse's flame.

Far from the madding crowd's ignoble strife,
 Their sober wishes never learn'd to stray;
Along the cool sequester'd vale of life
 They kept the noiseless tenor of their way.

Yet ev'n these bones from insult to protect,
 Some frail memorial still erected nigh,
With uncouth rhymes and shapeless sculpture deck'd,
 Implores the passing tribute of a sigh.

Their name, their years, spelt by th' unletter'd muse,
 The place of fame and elegy supply:
And many a holy text around she strews,
 That teach the rustic moralist to die.

For who to dumb Forgetfulness a prey,
    This pleasing anxious being e'er resign'd,
Left the warm precincts of the cheerful day,
    Nor cast one longing, ling'ring look behind?

On some fond breast the parting soul relies,
    Some pious drops the closing eye requires;
Ev'n from the tomb the voice of Nature cries,
    Ev'n in our ashes live their wonted fires.

For thee, who mindful of th' unhonour'd Dead
    Dost in these lines their artless tale relate;
If chance, by lonely contemplation led,
    Some kindred spirit shall inquire thy fate,

Haply some hoary-headed swain may say,
    'Oft have we seen him at the peep of dawn
Brushing with hasty steps the dews away
    To meet the sun upon the upland lawn.

'There at the foot of yonder nodding beech
    That wreathes its old fantastic roots so high,
His listless length at noontide would he stretch,
    And pore upon the brook that babbles by.

'Hard by yon wood, now smiling as in scorn,
    Mutt'ring his wayward fancies he would rove,
Now drooping, woeful wan, like one forlorn,
    Or craz'd with care, or cross'd in hopeless love.

'One morn I miss'd him on the custom'd hill,
    Along the heath and near his fav'rite tree;
Another came; nor yet beside the rill,
    Nor up the lawn, nor at the wood was he;

'The next with dirges due in sad array
    Slow thro' the church-way path we saw him borne.
Approach and read (for thou canst read) the lay,
    Grav'd on the stone beneath yon aged thorn.'

THE EPITAPH

Here rests his head upon the lap of Earth
    A youth to Fortune and to Fame unknown.
Fair Science frown'd not on his humble birth,
    And Melancholy mark'd him for her own.

Large was his bounty, and his soul sincere,
    Heav'n did a recompense as largely send:
He gave to Mis'ry all he had, a tear,
    He gained from Heav'n ('twas all he wish'd) a friend.

No farther from his merits to disclose,
    Or draw his frailties from their dread abode,
(There they alike in trembling hope repose)
    The bosom of his Father and his God.

                                                            Thomas Gray

Chosen by **Julian Lloyd Webber FRCM**, concert cellist: 'I have always loved
this poem's sense of peace, evoking the eighteenth-century countryside.'

BHAGAVATI[13]

Bhagavati ... Bhagavati ...

Planted together by the eternal giver
Two willow trees dipped and sipped
At the river of life.

Neither in the shadow of the other and yet
Both intermingled like wind that has met
Each one alone though inseparably bound
By the ground.

When death the compassionate giver arrives
Both fall in
And die.

Bhagavati ... Bhagavati ...

Barry Long

Chosen by **Barry Long**, spiritual teacher: 'The poem represents a spiritual reality which I have realized and devote my life to by endeavouring to impart the spirit of it to others.'

---

[13] *Bhagavati* = God in female form.

THE SEVENTH ANGEL

The seventh angel
is completely different
even his name is different
Szemkel

he is not like Gabriel
the golden
pillar on the throne
and baldachin

nor like Raphael
the choir-tuner

nor even
Azrael
engineer of the planets
geometer of infinity
splendid exponent of theoretical physics

Szemkel
is black and nervous
and has been fined many times for
illegal import of sinners

between the abyss
and the heavens
without a rest his feet go pit-a-pat

his sense of dignity is non-existent
and they only keep him in the squad
out of consideration for the number seven

but he is not like the others
not like the hetman of the hosts
Michael
all scales and feathery plumes

nor like Azrafael
interior decorator of the universe
warden of its luxuriant vegetation
his wings shimmering like two oak trees

nor even like
Dedrael
apologist and cabalist

Szemkel Szemkel
... the angels complain
why can't you be splendid?

the Byzantine artists
when they paint all seven
reproduce Szemkel
just like the rest

because they fear
they might lapse into heresy
if they were to portray him
just as he is
black nervous
with his old halo tarnished.

Zbigniew Herbert
(translated from the Polish by Peter Dale Scott)

Chosen by **Rabbi Professor Jonathan Magonet**, Principal of Leo Baeck College: 'The image of the seventh angel, with tarnished halo and often fined for "illegal import of sinners", clarified for me the quality of a number of people whom I experienced as my religious teachers. They are often on the margins of their religious organization because they are felt to be too dangerous to be given power – but without them the organization would lack any religion at all. So Szemkel has become for me the guardian angel of all sinner smugglers.'

THE SUNLIGHT ON THE GARDEN

The sunlight on the garden
Hardens and grows cold,
We cannot cage the minute
Within its nets of gold,
When all is told
We cannot beg for pardon.

Our freedom as free lances
Advances towards its end;
The earth compels, upon it
Sonnets and birds descend;
And soon, my friend,
We shall have no time for dances.

The sky was good for flying
Defying the church bells
And every evil iron
Siren and what it tells:
The earth compels,
We are dying, Egypt, dying

And not expecting pardon,
Hardened in heart anew,
But glad to have sat under
Thunder and rain with you,
And grateful too
For sunlight on the garden.

Louis MacNeice

Chosen by **Wolf Mankowitz**, author.

A HYMN TO GOD THE FATHER

Wilt thou forgive that sin where I begun,
Which was my sin, though it were done before?
Wilt thou forgive that sin; through which I run,
And do run still: though still I do deplore?
When thou hast done, thou hast not done,
For I have more.

Wilt thou forgive that sin which I have won
Others to sin? and, made my sin their door?
Wilt thou forgive that sin which I did shun
A year, or two: but wallowed in, a score?
When thou hast done, thou hast not done,
For I have more.

I have a sin of fear, that when I have spun
My last thread, I shall perish on the shore;
But swear by thy self, that at my death thy sun
Shall shine as he shines now, and heretofore;
And, having done that, thou hast done,
I fear no more.

John Donne

Chosen by the **Rt Hon. the Lord Menuhin OM KBE**, violinist and conductor:
'I am always revolted by the pointing of a finger at the accused – this usually
is to serve one's own feeling of innocence, superiority, blamelessness and
authority. Jesus must have thought that when he said "let him throw the first
stone" etc. We are so prone to condemn the Germans, Communists, Jews,
Muslims, Americans – in fact no people escape condemnation. It is so urgent
to realize that we are all to carry responsibility and guilt for the crimes of
mankind. This attitude has two advantages: (1) that we will correct these crimes
more early; (2) that we will show more compassion and understanding.'

THOU ART INDEED JUST, LORD

Thou art indeed just, Lord, if I contend
With thee; but, sir, so what I plead is just.
Why do sinners' ways prosper? and why must
Disappointment all I endeavour end?
    Wert thou my enemy, O thou my friend,
How wouldst thou worse, I wonder, than thou dost
Defeat, thwart me? Oh, the sots and thralls of lust
Do in spare hours more thrive than I that spend,
Sir, life upon thy cause. See, banks and brakes
Now, leavèd how thick! lacèd they are again
With fretty chervil, look, and fresh wind shakes
Them; birds build – but not I build; no, but strain,
Time's eunuch, and not breed one work that wakes.
Mine, O thou lord of life, send my roots rain.

Gerard Manley Hopkins

Chosen by **Deborah Moggach**, writer: 'A poem of heart-breaking desperation – like all great poems, it makes one feel companioned, even in the bleakest of circumstances.'

FROM IN MEMORIAM A.H.H.

CVI

Ring out, wild bells, to the wild sky,
    The flying cloud, the frosty light:
    The year is dying in the night;
Ring out, wild bells, and let him die.

Ring out the old, ring in the new,
    Ring, happy bells, across the snow:
    The year is going, let him go;
Ring out the false, ring in the true.

Ring out the grief that saps the mind,
    For those that here we see no more;
    Ring out the feud of rich and poor,
Ring in redress to all mankind.

Ring out a slowly dying cause,
    And ancient forms of party strife;
    Ring in the nobler modes of life,
With sweeter manners, purer laws.

Ring out the want, the care, the sin,
    The faithless coldness of the times;
    Ring out, ring out thy mournful rhymes,
But ring the fuller minstrel in.

Ring out false pride in place and blood,
    The civic slander and the spite;
    Ring in the love of truth and right,
Ring in the common love of good.

Ring out old shapes of foul disease;
    Ring out the narrowing lust of gold;
    Ring out the thousand wars of old,
Ring in the thousand years of peace.

Ring in the valiant man and free,
    The larger heart, the kindlier hand;
    Ring out the darkness of the land,
Ring in the Christ that is to be.

Alfred Lord Tennyson

Chosen by **Bel Mooney**, novelist, children's author and broadcaster: 'A friend faxed me this poem once when I was miserable, and I turn to it as a sublime statement of hope. Whatever the proofs to the contrary, humankind is capable of the greatest things, and I share the poet's optimism that our natural movement is, like flowers, towards the light.'

THE DONKEY

When fishes flew and forests walked
    And figs grew upon thorn,
Some moment when the moon was blood
    Then surely I was born.

With monstrous head and sickening cry
    And ears like errant wings,
The devil's walking parody
    On all four-footed things.

The tattered outlaw of the earth,
    Of ancient crooked will;
Starve, scourge, deride me: I am dumb,
    I keep my secret still.

Fools! For I also had my hour;
    One far fierce hour and sweet:
There was a shout about my ears,
    And palms before my feet.

G. K. Chesterton

Chosen by **Baroness Nicholson**, Liberal Democrat Peer: 'The donkey is synonymous with the Christian faith, and yet throughout the world it is abused with impunity, yet continues to be our beast of burden without complaint, as Christ carries our burdens.'

PREPARATIONS

Yet if His Majesty, our sovereign lord,
Should of his own accord
Friendly himself invite,
And say 'I'll be your guest to-morrow night,'
How should we stir ourselves, call and command
All hands to work! 'Let no man idle stand!
Set me fine Spanish tables in the hall;
See they be fitted all;
Let there be room to eat
And order taken that there want no meat.
See every sconce and candlestick made bright,
That without tapers they may give a light.
Look to the presence: are the carpets spread,
The dazie o'er the head,
The cushions in the chairs,
And all the candles lighted on the stairs?
Perfume the chambers, and in any case
Let each man give attendance in his place!'
Thus, if the king were coming, would we do;
And 'twere good reason too;
For 'tis a duteous thing
To show all honour to an earthly king,
And after all our travail and our cost,
So he be pleased, to think no labour lost.
But at the coming of the King of Heaven
All's set at six and seven;
We wallow in our sin,
Christ cannot find a chamber in the inn.
We entertain him always like a stranger,
And, as at first, still lodge him in the manger.

Anonymous

Chosen by **John Julius Norwich**, writer: 'This is one of my mother's favourite poems, which I have known by heart since childhood.'

FESTE'S SONG

When that I was and a little tiny boy,
   With hey, ho, the wind and the rain,
A foolish thing was but a toy,
   For the rain it raineth every day.

But when I came to man's estate,
   With hey, ho, the wind and the rain,
'Gainst knaves and thieves men shut their gate,
   For the rain it raineth every day.

But when I came, alas! to wive
   With hey, ho, the wind and the rain,
By swaggering could I never thrive,
   For the rain it raineth every day.

But when I came unto my beds,
   With hey, ho, the wind and the rain,
With toss-pots still had drunken heads,
   For the rain it raineth every day.

A great while ago the world begun,
   With hey, ho, the wind and the rain,
But that's all one, our play is done,
   And we'll strive to please you every day.

William Shakespeare
(Twelfth Night, Act V, Scene I, lines 398–417)

Chosen by **Robert Nye**, poet and novelist: 'I like it that Shakespeare gave fools some of his best lines. I think there is something both profoundly Christian and deeply true to the English spirit in this. Feste's song is to me as "spiritual" as anything to be found in Dante, yet speaking, as it were, through the senses, in the language of the body.'

WE HAVE FORGOTTEN THE NAMES

We have forgotten the names
We ignore the places
And the face of God
Lies unrecognised
in the fallow fields
Of our desecration

Become the flower
Of the rock's memory.
Be heard as the groan
Of the high mountains of the world
And in the curve
Of the straight line,
Behold your God.

Prue Fitzgerald

Chosen by **Martin Palmer**, Director of the International Consultancy on Religion, Education and Culture, head of the Sacred Land Project, and broadcaster: 'The lost landscapes of both our minds and of the actual land have left us with few signposts for either spirituality or a proper relationship with nature. Prue's poem challenges this and asks us to see the familiar landscapes around us and within, in a new light.'

THE GARDEN

How vainly men themselves amaze
To win the palm, the oak, or bays;
And their uncessant labours see
Crowned from some single herb or tree.
Whose short and narrow verged shade
Does prudently their toils upbraid;
While all flowers and all trees do close
To weave the garlands of repose.

Fair quiet, have I found thee here,
And innocence thy sister dear!
Mistaken long, I sought you then
In busy companies of men.
Your sacred plants, if here below,
Only among the plants will grow:
Society is all but rude,
To this delicious solitude.

No white nor red was ever seen
So am'rous as this lovely green.
Fond lovers, cruel as their flame,
Cut in these trees their mistress' name.
Little, alas, they know or heed,
How far these beauties hers exceed!
Fair trees! where s'eer your barks I wound,
No name shall but your own be found.

When we have run our passions' heat,
Love hither makes his best retreat.
The gods that mortal Beauty chase,
Still in a tree did end their race.
Apollo hunted Daphne so,
Only that she might laurel grow.
And Pan did after Syrinx speed,
Not as a nymph, but for a reed.

What wondrous life in this I lead!
Ripe apples drop about my head;
The luscious clusters of the vine
Upon my mouth do crush their wine;
The nectarine, and curious[14] peach,
Into my hands themselves do reach;
Stumbling on melons, as I pass,
Ensnared with flowers, I fall on grass.

Meanwhile the mind, from pleasure less,
Withdraws into its happiness:
The mind, that ocean where each kind
Does straight its own resemblance find;
Yet it creates, transcending these,
Far other worlds, and other seas;
Annihilating all that's made
To a green thought in a green shade.

---

[14] curious = exquisite

Here at the fountain's sliding foot,
Or at some fruit-tree's mossy root,
Casting the body's vest aside,
My soul into the boughs does glide:
There like a bird it sits, and sings,
Then whets,[15] and combs its silver wings;
And, till prepared for longer flight,
Waves in its plumes the various light.

Such was that happy garden-state,
While man there walked without a mate:
After a place so pure, and sweet,
What other help could yet be meet!
But 'twas beyond a mortal's share
To wander solitary there:
Two paradises 'twere in one.
To live in paradise alone.

How well the skilful gard'ner drew
Of flowers and herbs this dial new;
Where from above the milder sun
Does through a fragrant zodiac run;
And, as it works, the industrious bee
Computes its time as well as we.
How could such sweet and wholesome hours
Be reckoned but with herbs and flowers!

Andrew Marvell

Chosen by **Will Parfitt**, psychotherapist and author: 'This poem conveys the deep spiritual contentment that can be found in oneness with nature, along with the existential pain and longing inherent in the human experience of separation.'

---

[15] whets = preens

EPIRRHEMA

Always in observing nature
Look at one and every creature;
Nothing's outside that's not within,
For nature has no heart or skin.
All at once that way you'll see
The sacred open mystery.

True seeming is the joy it gives,
The joy of serious playing;
No thing is single, if it lives,
But multiple its being.

Johann Wolfgang von Goethe
(translated from the German by Michael Hamburger)

Chosen by **Sara Parkin**, Director of Forum for the Future: 'Briefly and simply this poem describes the complexity and interconnectedness of nature, the human being and a common, inspiring but mysterious spirituality – the very essence of that elusive concept, sustainability.'

FULL CIRCLE WORLD

Good morning dear world,
So briefly known.
In flashes only seen,
So often missed
By eyes so self-obsessed.
Good morning dear earth,
With your clouds like flags unfurled
And your sun that walks on beams of frost
And lights all we thought lost.
Good morning dear mist,
Dear floating lakes of light through which
The numbed bee and its cargo sails.
Good morning dear sky,
Dear scented woven threads of air
That blow away despair
From this world so briefly known,
In flashes only seen,
So often missed
By eyes so self-obsessed.
Good morning dear world.

Brian Patten

Chosen by **Brian Patten**, poet: '"Full Circle World" is an affirmation I'd written following a group of poems on my mother's death.'

THE GUESTHOUSE

A mere guesthouse is the state of our being
where every morning a new visitor comes to stay.
Each guest of your thoughts will bear you a gift –
it could be the sound of a calling,
or it may be a vision of heartache and pain.

My friend, leave your door open,
always the perfect host.
Wait patiently on the threshold
to meet your next caller.

The guests who come
from the world unknown
are to be welcomed
with an open heart.

Even though they may wreck your home,
don't turn them away,
lest they flee into
nothingness.

Jalaluddin Rumi
(translated from the Persian by Maryam Mafi)

Chosen by **Foster Perry**, spiritual teacher, author and President of the Hummingbird Foundation: 'Life can be a dark, cavernous existence, but Rumi enlightens the guest and lights a candle in the darkness and complexity of the soul. Through his teaching I have learned gratitude for the shadows, and laughed them in and invited healing into the home of the Beloved.'

LEAD, KINDLY LIGHT

Lead, kindly Light! amid the encircling gloom,
Lead thou me on;
The night is dark, and I am far from home,
Lead thou me on:
Keep thou my feet; I do not ask to see
The distant scene; one step enough for me.

John Henry Newman

Chosen by **Robert M. Pirsig**, author: 'If one can describe the hymn "Lead, Kindly Light" as religious poetry set to music, then it is the best religious poem I know. What first recommended it to me was the fact that Mohandas Gandhi considered it his favourite hymn, indicating a universality for it that not all hymns (such as "Onward Christian Soldiers") can claim. In my second book, *Lila*, this was expounded on a little:

'In other cultures, or in religious literature of our past, where the immune system of "objectivity" is weak or non-existent, reference to this light is everywhere, from the Protestant hymn "Lead, Kindly Light", to the halos of the saints. The central terms of Western mysticism, "enlightenment", and "illumination" refer to it directly. *Darsana*, a fundamental Hindu form of religious instruction, means "giving of light". Descriptions of Zen *satori* mention it. It is referred to extensively in *The Tibetan Book of the Dead*.'

ODE TO THE WEST WIND

I

O Wild West Wind, thou breath of Autumn's being
Thou from whose unseen presence the leaves dead
Are driven like ghosts from an enchanter fleeing,

Yellow, and black, and pale, and hectic red,
Pestilence-stricken multitudes! O thou
Who chariotest to their dark wintry bed

The wingèd seeds, where they lie cold and low,
Each like a corpse within its grave, until
Thine azure sister of the Spring shall blow

Her clarion o'er the dreaming earth, and fill
(Driving sweet buds like flocks to feed in air)
With living hues and odours plain and hill;

Wild Spirit, which art moving everywhere;
Destroyer and preserver; hear, O hear!

II

Thou on whose stream, 'mid the steep sky's commotion,
Loose clouds like earth's decaying leaves are shed,
Shook from the tangled boughs of heaven and ocean,

Angels of rain and lightning! there are spread
On the blue surface of thine airy surge,
Like the bright hair uplifted from the head

Of some fierce Mænad, even from the dim verge
Of the horizon to the zenith's height,
The locks of the approaching storm. Thou dirge

Of the dying year, to which this closing night
Will be the dome of a vast sepulchre,
Vaulted with all thy congregated might

Of vapours, from whose solid atmosphere
Black rain, and fire, and hail, will burst: O hear!

III

Thou who didst waken from his summer dreams
The blue Mediterranean, where he lay,
Lull'd by the coil of his crystalline streams,

Beside a pumice isle in Baiæ's bay,
And saw in sleep old palaces and towers
Quivering within the wave's intenser day,

All overgrown with azure moss, and flowers
So sweet, the sense faints picturing them! Thou
For whose path the Atlantic's level powers

Cleave themselves into chasms, while far below
The sea-blooms and the oozy woods which wear
The sapless foliage of the ocean, know

Thy voice, and suddenly grow gray with fear,
And tremble and despoil themselves: O hear!

IV

If I were a dead leaf thou mightest bear;
If I were a swift cloud to fly with thee;
A wave to pant beneath thy power, and share

The impulse of thy strength, only less free
Than thou, O uncontrollable! if even
I were as in my boyhood, and could be

The comrade of thy wanderings over heaven,
As then, when to outstrip thy skiey speed
Scarce seem'd a vision – I would ne'er have striven

As thus with thee in prayer in my sore need.
O! lift me as a wave, a leaf, a cloud!
I fall upon the thorns of life! I bleed!

A heavy weight of hours has chain'd and bow'd
One too like thee – tameless, and swift, and proud.

v

Make me thy lyre, even as the forest is:
What if my leaves are falling like its own?
The tumult of thy mighty harmonies

Will take from both a deep autumnal tone,
Sweet though in sadness. Be thou, Spirit fierce,
My spirit! Be thou me, impetuous one!

Drive my dead thoughts over the universe,
Like wither'd leaves, to quicken a new birth;
And, by the incantation of this verse,

Scatter, as from an unextinguish'd hearth
Ashes and sparks, my words among mankind!
Be through my lips to unawaken'd earth

The trumpet of a prophecy! O Wind,
If Winter comes, can Spring be far behind?

Percy Bysshe Shelley

Chosen by **Kathleen Raine**, poet: 'I would name this poem, whose theme is inspiration itself, under the worldwide and immemorial symbol of "wind" or "breath" of the spirit. This symbol is found within the Jewish-Christian scriptures themselves, as God "breathed into man the breath of life" or the "wind that blows where it listeth; man heareth the sound thereof and it is gone". Shelley was, of course, a Platonist. By means of a sequence of images taken from nature – dead leaves from the "pestilence-stricken multitudes" of suffering mankind; the inspiration of the Mænads in the "locks of the approaching storms"; the living seeds of the future; the sparks of fire among the ashes; ending with the explicit prayer of the poet for inspiration, "Be thou, spirit fierce! my spirit, be thou me, impetuous one!" – the poet as "the trumpet of prophecy" is discoursing on the theme of inspiration from a higher, divine source. At all points the descriptive level of the poem is gloriously realistic, but it resonates at the higher levels of the vertical dimension of the soul, and beyond that the metaphysical. Because our age has lost the art of reading natural symbols as a language in which poets have traditionally discoursed on the meanings and experiences of the soul and the realities of the cosmos, we can no longer read such poems unless we relearn. A great deal of English poetry of the past 200 years – including the great bulk of popular contemporary verse – uses language to describe nature; whereas great poets employ nature as a language to speak of the spiritual order of meaning and experience of the higher worlds.'

FROM TRANSMISSIONS

XXIV

I saw a great light come down over London,
And buildings and cars and people were still
They were held wherever they were under the sky's
Clear humming radiance as it descended –
Everywhere, in shops, behind desks and on trains
Everything stopped as the stillness came down
And touched the crown of our heads
As our eyes closed, and the sky filled us,
And our minds became the sky –
And everyone, regardless of crime class or creed
Was touched; as slowly we began to stir
Out of this penetrated light-filled sleep
Dizzily as the hand completed its dialling,
And the train lurched forward
And I saw faces looking at one another questioning,
I saw people meeting eye to eye and standing
Half-amazed by each other's presence
I saw their mouths silently shaping the word *why*
Why didn't we know this? And yet knowing
They already knew, and without words
We all stood searching for the gesture
That would say it –

As the lights went green, and we drove on.

Jay Ramsay

Chosen by **Jay Ramsay**, poet, therapist, workshop leader and lecturer: 'Why is this poem meaningful? For me it expresses something of the potency of light that is available at an essential level beyond our minds, and is as palpably real as physical sunlight. The poem takes place at a set of traffic lights: in those moments of waiting, whether by chance or design, we can open up to the larger reality we are a part of, which sustains us infinitely more than we tend to recognize.'

FROM LEAVES OF GRASS

This is what you shall do: love the earth and sun and the animals, despise riches, give alms to everyone that asks, stand up for the stupid and crazy, devote your income and labour to others, hate tyrants, argue not concerning God, have patience and indulgence toward the people, take off your hat to nothing known or unknown or to any man or number of men ... re-examine all you have been told at church or school or in any book, dismiss whatever insults your own soul and your very flesh shall be a great poem.

Walt Whitman
(from the Introduction to Leaves of Grass*)*

Chosen by **Anita Roddick OBE**, Founder and Chief Executive of The Body Shop: 'This poem means a great deal to me because it reminds me of my mother. My mother pushed me to the edge of bravery. She challenged everything and she created a world that allowed my spirit to flourish. Every time I did anything kind or loving to anyone, she would delight in it. From day one I was told my genetic pattern was to have a bold spirit, and to create a world that enabled the spirit to flourish.'

JOY OF MY LIFE! WHILE LEFT ME HERE

Joy of my life! While left me here,
    And still my love!
How in thy absence thou dost steer
    Me from above!
    A life well led
    This truth commends.
    With quick, or dead
    It never ends.

Stars are of mighty use: The night
    Is dark, and long;
The road foul, and where one goes right,
    Six may go wrong.
    One twinkling ray
    Shot o'er some cloud
    May clear much way
    And guide a crowd.

God's saints are shining lights: who stays
    Here long must pass
O'er dark hills, swift streams, and steep ways
    As smooth as glass;
    But they all night
    Like candles, shed
    Their beams, and light
    Us into bed.

They are (indeed) our pillar-fires
        Seen as we go,
They are that city's shining spires
        We travel to;
        A swordlike gleam
        Kept man for sin
        First *out*; this beam
        Will guide him *in*.

Henry Vaughan

Chosen by **Cicely Saunders OM, DBE, FRCP**, Chairman and Founder of St Christopher's Hospice: 'This poem is one I learnt by heart in a period of bereavement. It was a help and an inspiration at a difficult time.'

DEATH STANDS ABOVE ME

Death stands above me, whispering low
   I know not what into my ear:
Of his strange language all I know
   Is, there is not a word of fear.

Walter Savage Landor

Chosen by **Ned Sherrin**, presenter, writer and director: 'This is the frame of mind in which I would hope to approach death – which grows increasingly near.'

TIEME RANAPIRI ('MY LAW')

The sun may be clouded, yet ever the sun
Will sweep on its course till the Cycle is run.
And when into chaos the system is hurled
Again shall the Builder reshape a new world.

Your path may be clouded, uncertain your goal:
Move on – for your orbit is fixed to your soul.
And though it may lead into darkness of night
The torch of the Builder shall give it new light.

You were. You will be! Know this while you are:
Your spirit has travelled both long and afar.
It came from the Source, to the Source it returns –
The Spark which was lighted eternally burns.

It slept in a jewel. It leapt in a wave.
It roamed in the forest. It rose from the grave.
It took on strange garbs for long aeons of years
And now in the soul of yourself It appears.

From body to body your spirit speeds on
It seeks a new form when the old one has gone
And the form that it finds in the fabric you wrought
On the loom of the Mind from the fibre of Thought.

As dew is drawn upwards, in rain to descend
Your thoughts drift away and in Destiny blend.
You cannot escape them, for petty or great,
Or evil or noble, they fashion your Fate.

Somewhere on some planet, sometime and somehow
Your life will reflect your thoughts of your Now.
My Law is unerring, no blood can atone –
The structure you built you will live in – alone.

From cycle to cycle, through time and through space
Your lives with your longings will ever keep pace
And all that you ask for, and all you desire
Must come at your bidding, as flame out of fire.

Once list to that Voice and all tumult is done –
Your life is the Life of the Infinite One.
In the hurrying race you are conscious of pause
With love for the purpose, and love for the Cause.

You are your own Devil, you are your own God
You fashioned the paths your footsteps have trod.
And no-one can save you from Error or Sin
Until you have hark'd to the Spirit within.

Anonymous
(translator from the Maori unknown)

Chosen by **Betty Shine**, medium, healer and author: 'Through my work I have found this poem encapsulates the whole truth enabling one to confront the enemy within – and win.'

A HYMN

O God of earth and altar,
    Bow down and hear our cry,
Our earthly rulers falter,
    Our people drift and die;
The walls of gold entomb us,
    The swords of scorn divide,
Take not thy thunder from us,
    But take away our pride.

From all that terror teaches,
    From lies of tongue and pen,
From all the easy speeches
    That comfort cruel men,
For sale and profanation
    Of honour and the sword,
From sleep and from damnation,
    Deliver us, good Lord.

Tie in a living tether
    The prince and priest and thrall,
Bind all our lives together,
    Smite us and save us all;
In ire and exultation
    Aflame with faith, and free,
Lift up a living nation,
    A single sword to thee.

G. K. Chesterton

Chosen by **Edward de Souza**, actor: 'It is my Hymn of Hymns and a conscience-scouring prayer. If the world would sing it and pray it, what a world it would be.'

A MAN'S A MAN FOR A' THAT

Is there, for honest poverty
That hangs his head, and a' that;
The coward-slave, we pass him by,
   We dare be poor for a' that!
For a' that, and a' that,
   Our toils obscure, and a' that,
The rank is but the guinea's stamp,
   The man's the gowd[16] for a' that.

What though on hamely[17] fare we dine,
   Wear hoddin grey,[18] and a' that;
Gie[19] fools their silks, and knaves their wine,
   A man's a man for a' that:
For a' that, and a' that,
   Their tinsel show, and a' that;
The honest man, though e'er sae[20] poor,
   Is king o' men for a' that.

---

[16] gowd = gold

[17] hamely = homely

[18] hoddin = coarse wool

[19] gie = give

[20] sae = so

Ye see yon birkie,[21] ca'd[22] a lord,
    Wha struts, and stares, and a' that;
Though hundreds worship at his word,
    He's but a coof[23] for a' that:
For a' that, and a' that,
    His ribband,[24] star, and a' that,
The man of independent mind,
    He looks and laughs at a' that.

A prince can mak a belted knight,
    A marquis, duke, and a' that;
But an honest man's aboon[25] his might,
    Gude[26] faith, he mauna fa'[27] that!
For a' that, and a' that,
    Their dignities, and a' that,
The pith o' sense, and pride o' worth,
    Are higher ranks than a' that.

---

[21] birkie = fellow
[22] ca'd = called
[23] coof = idiot
[24] ribband = ribbon
[25] aboon = above
[26] gude = good
[27] mauna fa' = must not lay claim to

Then let us pray that come it may,
　　As come it will for a' that,
That sense and worth, o'er a' the earth,
　　May bear the gree,[28] and a' that.
For a' that, and a' that,
Its comin yet for a' that,
That man to man, the warld o'er,
Shall brothers be for a' that.

Robert Burns

Chosen by **David, the Rt Hon. Lord Steel of Aikwood**, former Liberal leader: 'This poem is a powerful appeal for the brotherhood of man.'

---

[28] bear the gree = have the first place

BEATITUDE

Blessed are the flabby people at Walgreen's
buying Trojan transparent ribbed golden condoms.

Unlike the couple on the package,
they have never had
a beach encounter at sunset.

They are landlocked.
They have shoveled their weight in worries
and are well acquainted with mulch.

They have problems with flatulence
because they fry with lard.

Yet darkness
rocks their unfashionable limbs
into phosphorescence.

In that tide they overcome gravity.
Holy, they vocalize with the whales.

Claire Bateman

Chosen by **Brother David Steindl-Rast OSB**, author, Benedictine monk and hermit: 'This poem reveals with unabashed compassion the sacred nature of our bodies and of sexuality. We need reminding. Immersed in mysteries, we may fail to be aware what sacred rituals we are performing. Abraham Heschel said: "Just to be, is holy."'

WONDER

How like an angel came I down!
　　How bright are all things here!
When first among his works I did appear,
　　Oh, how their Glory me did crown!
The world resembled his Eternity,
　　In which my soul did walk;
　　And every thing that I did see
　　Did with me talk.

The skies in their magnificence,
　　The lively, lovely air;
Oh, how divine, how soft, how sweet, how fair!
　　The stars did entertain my sense,
And all the works of God so bright and pure,
　　So rich and great did seem
　　As if they ever must endure
　　In my esteem.

A native health and innocence
　　Within my bones did grow,
And while my God did all his glories show,
　　I felt a vigour in my sense
That was all spirit. I within did flow
　　With seas of life, like wine;
　　I nothing in the world did know,
　　But 'twas divine.

Harsh, ragged objects were concealed,
    Oppressions, tears, and cries,
Sins, griefs, complaints, dissentions, weeping eyes,
    Were hid: and only things revealed
Which heavenly spirits and the angels prize.
    The State of Innocence
And Bliss, not trades and poverties,
    Did fill my sense.

The streets were paved with golden stones,
    The boys and girls were mine;
Oh, how did all their lovely faces shine!
    The Sons of Men were Holy Ones,
Joy, Beauty, Welfare did appear to me,
    And every thing which here I found,
While like an angel I did see,
    Adorned the ground.

Rich diamond, and pearl, and gold
    In every place was seen;
Rare splendours, yellow, blue, red, white, and green,
    Mine eyes did everywhere behold;
Great Wonders clothed with Glory did appear,
    Amazement was my Bliss.
That and my wealth was everywhere:
    No Joy to this ...

Thomas Traherne

TO THE SPIRIT

Give me purity of will,
Not for hope of heaven,
Rather for *this* Now,
That I may do no evil
But present our LIGHT
In lightness, smiles,
Understandings, joys.
So doing, my short life
Will be theirs and ours.

Robert Tear

Chosen by **Robert Tear**, opera singer: 'The first poem, "Wonder" by Thomas Traherne, perfectly expresses how the world appears when the soul is released of the self and occupies its true position of *joy* in the *all*. The tenor of the second verse, "To the Spirit", is the importance of the Holy Now and the conspiracy between God and myself to show it to others.'

WHEN YOU ARE OLD

When you are old and grey and full of sleep,
And nodding by the fire, take down this book,
And slowly read, and dream of the soft look
Your eyes had once, and of their shadows deep;

How many loved your moments of glad grace,
And loved your beauty with love false or true,
But one man loved the pilgrim soul in you,
And loved the sorrows of your changing face;

And bending down beside the glowing bars,
Murmur, a little sadly, how Love fled
And paced upon the mountains overhead
And hid his face amid a crowd of stars.

W. B. Yeats

Chosen by **Leslie Thomas**, author: 'The saddest thing about a happy marriage is that, at some time, one person must be left behind. I think this is a poem of great comfort and love.'

TALIESIN AND THE SPRING OF VISION

'I tread the sand at the sea's edge, sand of the hour-glass,
And the sand receives my footprint, singing:
"You are my nearmost, you who have travelled the farthest,
And you are my constant, who have endured all vicissitudes
In the cradle of the sea, Fate's hands, and the spinning waters.
The measure of past grief is the measure of present joy.
Your tears, which have dried to Chance, now spring from a secret.
Here time's glass breaks, and the world is transfigured in music."'

So sang the grains of sand, and while they whirled to a pattern
Taliesin took refuge under the unfledged rock.
He could not see in the cave, but groped with his hand,
And the rock he touched was the socket of all men's eyes,
And he touched the spring of vision. He had the mind of a fish
That moment. He knew the glitter of scale and fin.
He touched the pin of pivotal space, and he saw
One sandgrain balance the ages' cumulus cloud.

Earth's shadow hung. Taliesin said: 'The penumbra of history is terrible.
Life changes, breaks, scatters. There is no sheet-anchor.
Time reigns; yet the kingdom of love is every moment,
Whose citizens do not age in each other's eyes.
In a time of darkness the pattern of life is restored
By men who make all transience seem an illusion
Through inward acts, acts corresponding to music.
Their works of love leave words that do not end in the heart.'

He still held rock. Then three drops fell on his fingers,
And Future and Past converged in a lightning flash:
'It was we who instructed Shakespeare, who fell upon Dante's eyes,
Who opened to Blake the Minute Particulars. We are the soul's rebirth.'
Taliesin answered: 'I have encountered the irreducible diamond
In the rock. Yet now it is over. Omniscience is not for man.
Christen me, therefore, that my acts in the dark may be just,
And adapt my partial vision to the limitation of time.'

Vernon Watkins

Chosen by **R. S. Thomas**, poet: 'This is a visionary poem and is dateless, despite the contemporary tyranny of science and technology.'

PLEASE CALL ME BY MY TRUE NAMES

Don't say that I will depart tomorrow –
even today I am still arriving.

Look deeply: every second I am arriving
to be a bud on a Spring branch,
to be a tiny bird, with still-fragile wings,
learning to sing in my new nest,
to be a caterpillar in the heart of a flower,
to be a jewel hiding itself in a stone.

I still arrive, in order to laugh and to cry,
to fear and to hope.
The rhythm of my heart is the birth and death
of all that is alive.

I am a mayfly metamorphosing
on the surface of the river.
And I am the bird
that swoops down to swallow the mayfly.

I am the frog swimming happily
in the clear water of a pond.
And I am the grass-snake
that silently feeds itself on the frog.

I am the child in Uganda, all skin and bones,
my legs as thin as bamboo sticks.
And I am the arms merchant,
selling deadly weapons to Uganda.

I am the twelve-year-old girl,
refugee on a small boat,
who throws herself into the ocean
after being raped by a sea pirate.

And I am the pirate,
my heart not yet capable
of seeing and loving.

I am a member of the politburo,
with plenty of power in my hands.
And I am the man who has to pay
his 'debt of blood' to my people
dying slowly in a forced-labour camp.

My joy is like Spring, so warm
it makes flowers bloom all over the Earth.
My pain is like a river of tears,
so vast it fills the four oceans.

Please call me by my true names,
so I can hear all my cries and laughter at once,
so I can see that my joy and pain are one.

Please call me by my true names,
so I can wake up
and the door of my heart
could be left open,
the door of compassion.

Thich Nhat Hanh

Chosen by **Christopher Titmuss**, co-founder of Gaia House, member of the International Board of the Buddhist Peace Fellowship, and teacher of awakening and insight meditation: 'We live in a world under constant pressure of "I", "me" and "mine". In a moving and dramatic form, this poem reminds us that we all share the experience of "I". We have much more in common than we think. Let us never waver from this perception.'

SWEETNESS IN BITTERNESS

Is there a rose that smiles all the while?
A beauty that's ever the same?
Our destiny is to cry sometimes
So we will remember God's name.

Deep, the wells the world is crowded with.
If we are like Joseph our fate is to fall,
But falling, we find ourselves sat upon high –
May Love reach a hand to us all.

Worldly things mean a loss or a gain,
Around every rose is a barb.
In tartness there's sweetness, in hurt can be joy –
May suffering flavour your heart.

Let's turn pain into sherbet and drink,
Patiently cross the path of our woes.
May God grant us hunger for His pure love
So it can answer our moans.

The nut is cracked and dipped in honey,
The shell is thrown in the fire,
The lover is sold, in the market, to love
So Hüseyin can answer your cries.

Hüseyin Top
(translated from the Turkish by Kayhan Alsaç and Nigel Watts)

Chosen by **al-Haj Sheikh Hüseyin Top**, Sertariq of the Mevlevi Order: 'As food gains flavour and becomes edible through cooking, so people can be cooked and matured through pain. Sorrow and joy are twins; he who does not know sorrow cannot recognize and find joy. Everything materializes with its opposite. If what we call pain leads us to joy, then pain is not evil – on the contrary, that pain is goodness itself. If an illness brings someone closer to God, to divine values, that cannot be bad. An illness can be the remedy itself. Unless you crack the walnut shell open, you won't get to the kernel; without crushing an almond you won't get its oil. Wherever there is suffering we find God's compassion. You may prick yourself when you smell a rose, but then you refresh yourself with its beautiful scent.'

A LETTER TO JOHN DONNE

*Note: on 27 July, 1617, Donne preached at the parish church at Sevenoaks, of
which he was the rector, and was entertained at Knole, then the country residence
of Richard Sackville, third Earl of Dorset.*

I understand you well enough, John Donne
First, that you were a man of ability
Eaten by lust and by the love of God
Then, that you crossed the Sevenoaks High Street
As rector of Saint Nicholas:
I am of that parish.

To be a man of ability is not much
you may see them on the Sevenoaks platform any day
Eager men with despatch cases
Whom ambition drives as they drive the machine
Whom the certainty of meticulous operation
Pleasures as a morbid sex a heart of stone.

That you could have spent your time in the corruption of courts
As these in that of cities, gives you no place among us:
Ability is not even the game of a fool
But the click of a computer operating in a waste
Your cleverness is dismissed from this suit
Bring out your genitals and your theology.

What makes you familiar is this dual obsession;
Lust is not what the rutting stag knows
It is to take Eve's apple and to lose
The stag's paradisal look:
The love of God comes readily
To those who have most need.

You brought body and soul to this church
Walking there through the park alive with deer
But now what animal has climbed into your pulpit?
One whose pretension is that the fear
Of God has heated him into a spirit
An evaporated man no physical ill can hurt.

Well might you hesitate at the Latin gate
Seeing such apes denying the church of God:
I am grateful particularly that you were not a saint
But extravagant whether in bed or in your shroud.
You would understand that in the presence of folly
I am not sanctified but angry.

Come down and speak to the men of ability
On the Sevenoaks platform and tell them
That at your Saint Nicholas the faith
Is not exclusive in the fools it chooses
That the vain, the ambitious and the highly sexed
Are the natural prey of the incarnate Christ.

C. H. Sisson

Chosen by **Mark Tully**, journalist and broadcaster: 'I have so many favourite poems, but perhaps for today I would choose this one. It's a timely warning against relying on "ability" to give meaning to life – the arrogance of the "able". It's an attack on the present management culture which has dehumanized our institutions and takes pleasure only in "the certainty of meticulous operation". For me the unsolved mystery of life has been to live with lust and theology, yet I know I have been the "prey of the incarnate Christ".'

MUSÉE DES BEAUX ARTS

About suffering they were never wrong,
The Old Masters: how well they understood
Its human position; how it takes place
While someone else is eating or opening a window or just
walking dully along;
How, when the aged are reverently, passionately waiting
For the miraculous birth, there always must be
Children who did not specially want it to happen, skating
On a pond at the edge of the wood:
They never forgot
That even the dreadful martyrdom must run its course
Anyhow in a corner, some untidy spot
Where the dogs go on with their doggy life and the torturer's horse
Scratches its innocent behind on a tree.
In Brueghel's *Icarus*, for instance: how everything turns away
Quite leisurely from the disaster; the ploughman may
Have heard the splash, the forsaken cry,
But for him it was not an important failure; the sun shone
As it had to on the white legs disappearing into the green
Water; and the expensive delicate ship that must have seen
Something amazing, a boy falling out of the sky,
Had somewhere to get to and sailed calmly on.

W. H. Auden

Chosen by **Sir Stephen Tumim**, Principal of St Edmund Hall, Oxford: 'This poem is crisp and magical, and makes a series of comments on human life without pomposity or obscurity. It also comments separately on an important painting: a comment which I have never seen elsewhere.'

THE SILENT SELF

Silence is
   sitting still
   standing still
   lying still
consciously
   gratefully
     gracefully
breathing
inspiring –
   being inspired with life
       and love
   from him from whom these
     gifts do come –
the Lord of life and love –
the living Lord Jesus.

And in the stillness
     knowing
     and joyfully acknowledging
   that in Jesus alone
the silence of life and love is found.

Then to humbly rest
     sit
   stand
 lie
to bow the knee
in all that satisfying silence –
   and be fulfilled.

Harry Alfred Wiggett

Chosen by **Archbishop Desmond Tutu**: 'This poem was written by a friend, the Revd Harry Wiggett. I have a very special place in my heart for these particular words, which convey a strong feeling of serenity; a serene security which stems from knowing and loving God.'

THE BRIGHT FIELD

I have seen the sun break through
to illuminate a small field
for a while, and gone my way
and forgotten it. But that was the pearl
of great price, the one field that had
the treasure in it. I realise now
that I must give all that I have
to possess it. Life is not hurrying

on to a receding future, nor hankering after
an imagined past. It is the turning
aside like Moses to the miracle
of the lit bush, to a brightness
that seemed as transitory as your youth
once, but is the eternity that awaits you.

R. S. Thomas

Chosen by **Tim Waterstone**, Founder, Chairman and Chief Executive of Waterstone's Booksellers Ltd: 'Why is this poem meaningful to me? It's what I believe.'

LINES WRITTEN A FEW MILES ABOVE
TINTERN ABBEY

Five years have passed; five summers with the length
Of five long winters! and again I hear
These waters, rolling from their mountain-springs
With a sweet inland murmur. – Once again
Do I behold these steep and lofty cliffs,
Which on a wild and secluded scene impress
Thoughts of more deep seclusion; and connect
The landscape with the quiet of the sky.
The day is come when I again repose
Here, under this dark sycamore, and view
These plots of cottage-ground, these orchard-tufts,
Which, at this season, with their unripe fruits,
Among the woods and copses lose themselves,
Nor, with their green and simple hue, disturb
The wild green landscape. Once again I see
These hedge-rows, hardly hedge-rows, little lines
Of sportive wood run wild; these pastoral farms
Green to the very door; and wreathes of smoke
Sent up, in silence, from among the trees,
With some uncertain notice, as might seem,
Of vagrant dwellers in the houseless woods,
Or of some hermit's cave, where by his fire
The hermit sits alone.

               Though absent long,
These forms of beauty have not been to me,
As is a landscape to a blind man's eye:
But oft, in lonely rooms, and mid the din
Of towns and cities, I have owed to them,
In hours of weariness, sensations sweet,
Felt in the blood, and felt along the heart,
And passing even into my purer mind
With tranquil restoration: – feelings too

Of unremembered pleasure; such, perhaps,
As may have had no trivial influence
On that best portion of a good man's life;
His little, nameless, unremembered acts
Of kindness and of love. Nor less, I trust,
To them I may have owed another gift,
Of aspect more sublime; that blessed mood,
In which the burthen of the mystery,
In which the heavy and the weary weight
Of all this unintelligible world
Is lighten'd: – that serene and blessed mood,
In which the affections gently lead us on,
Until, the breath of this corporeal frame,
And even the motion of our human blood
Almost suspended, we are laid asleep
In body, and become a living soul:
While with an eye made quiet by the power
Of harmony, and the deep power of joy,
We see into the life of things.

                           If this
Be but a vain belief, yet, oh! how oft,
In darkness, and amid the many shapes
Of joyless day-light; when the fretful stir
Unprofitable, and the fever of the world,
Have hung upon the beatings of my heart,
How oft, in spirit, have I turned to thee
O sylvan Wye! Thou wanderer through the woods,
How often has my spirit turned to thee!

And now, with gleams of half-extinguish'd thought,
With many recognitions dim and faint,
And somewhat of a sad perplexity,
The picture of the mind revives again:
While here I stand, not only with the sense
Of present pleasure, but with pleasing thoughts

That in this moment there is life and food
For future years. And so I dare to hope
Though changed, no doubt, from what I was, when first
I came among these hills; when like a roe
I bounded o'er the mountains, by the sides
Of the deep rivers, and the lonely streams,
Wherever nature led; more like a man
Flying from something that he dreads, than one
Who sought the thing he loved. For nature then
(The coarser pleasures of my boyish days,
And their glad animal movements all gone by,)
To me was all in all. I cannot paint
What then I was. The sounding cataract
Haunted me like a passion: the tall rock,
The mountain, and the deep and gloomy wood,
Their colours and their forms, were then to me
An appetite: a feeling and a love,
That had no need of a remoter charm,
By thought supplied, or any interest
Unborrowed from the eye. – That time is past,
And all its aching joys are now no more,
And all its dizzy raptures. Not for this
Faint I, nor mourn nor murmur: other gifts
Have followed, for such loss, I would believe,
Abundant recompense. For I have learned
To look on nature, not as in the hour
Of thoughtless youth, but hearing oftentimes
The still, sad music of humanity,
Nor harsh nor grating, though of ample power
To chasten and subdue. And I have felt
A presence that disturbs me with the joy
Of elevated thoughts; a sense sublime
Of something far more deeply interfused,
Whose dwelling is the light of setting suns,
And the round ocean, and the living air,
And the blue sky, and in the mind of man,

A motion and a spirit, that impels
All thinking things, all objects of all thought,
And rolls through all things. Therefore am I still
A lover of the meadows and the woods,
And mountains; and of all that we behold
From this green earth; of all the mighty world
Of eye and ear, both what they half-create,
And what perceive; well pleased to recognize
In nature and the language of the sense,
The anchor of my purest thoughts, the nurse,
The guide, the guardian of my heart, and soul
Of all my moral being.

            Nor, perchance,
If I were not thus taught, should I the more
Suffer my genial spirits to decay:
For thou art with me, here, upon the banks
Of this fair river; thou, my dearest Friend,
My dear, dear Friend, and in thy voice I catch
The language of my former heart, and read
My former pleasures in the shooting lights
Of thy wild eyes. Oh! yet a little while
May I behold in thee what I was once,
My dear, dear Sister! And this prayer I make,
Knowing that Nature never did betray
The heart that loved her; 'tis her privilege,
Through all the years of this our life, to lead
From joy to joy: for she can so inform
The mind that is within us, so impress
With quietness and beauty, and so feed
With lofty thoughts, that neither evil tongues,
Rash judgements, not the sneers of selfish men,
Nor greetings where no kindness is, nor all
The dreary intercourse of daily life,
Shall e'er prevail against us, or disturb
Our cheerful faith that all which we behold

Is full of blessings. Therefore let the moon
Shine on thee in thy solitary walk;
And let the misty mountain winds be free
To blow against thee: and in after years,
When these wild ecstasies shall be matured
Into a sober pleasure, when thy mind
Shall be a mansion for all lovely forms,
Thy memory be as a dwelling-place
For all sweet sounds and harmonies; Oh! then,
If solitude, or fear, or pain, or grief,
Should be thy portion, with what healing thoughts
Of tender joy wilt thou remember me,
And these my exhortations! Nor, perchance,
If I should be, where I no more can hear
Thy voice, nor catch from thy wild eyes these gleams
Of past existence, wilt thou then forget
That on the banks of this delightful stream
We stood together; and that I, so long
A worshipper of Nature, hither came,
Unwearied in that service: rather say
With warmer love, oh! with far deeper zeal
Of holier love. Nor wilt thou then forget,
That after many wanderings, many years
Of absence, these steep woods and lofty cliffs,
And this green pastoral landscape, were to me
More dear, both for themselves, and for thy sake.

William Wordsworth

Chosen by **Nigel Watts**, novelist: 'This poem is special to me for many reasons: I know the Wye valley, and can imagine myself where Wordsworth stood, high above the river, looking through the woods. It is also special as a beautiful artefact with so many memorable lines – one of the greatest poems of one of the greatest poets. It is mainly precious to me, though, because of the company it kept me during a period in which I was searching for others who felt as I did. For many years I could not bring myself to believe in God, and yet neither could I deny the tug I felt towards spiritual matters. I discovered this poem during that period, and it exactly voiced my own recognition and celebration of this "presence". Nowhere is God mentioned (though of course, mentioned in every line, depending on the reader); there are no churches, no dogma, no belief. But neither is it just nature worship – either sentimentalized or self-righteously bucolic. This is a poem about seeing into the life of things, and discovering that such insight brings food on which we can live in the dreary, disconnected times.'

INTO THE HOUR

I have come into the hour of a white healing.
Grief's surgery is over and I wear
The scar of my remorse and of my feeling.

I have come into a sudden sunlit hour
When ghosts are scared to corners. I have come
Into the time when grief begins to flower

Into a new love. It had filled the room
Long before I recognised it. Now
I speak its name. Grief finds its good way home.

The apple-blossom's handsome on the bough
And Paradise spreads round. I touch its grass.
I want to celebrate but don't know how.

I need not speak though everyone I pass
Stares at me kindly. I would put my hand
Into their hands. Now I have lost my loss

In some way I may later understand.
I hear the singing of the summer grass.
And love, I find, has no considered end,

Nor is it subject to the wilderness
Which follows death. I am not traitor to
A person or a memory. I trace

Behind that love another which is running
Around, ahead. I need not ask its meaning.

Elizabeth Jennings

Chosen by **Dr Pauline M. Webb**, broadcaster and writer: 'I find that Elizabeth Jennings so often speaks to my immediate need. I read this poem just after a dear friend had died and I was trying to cope with the pangs of bereavement. The poem reminds us that life goes on, the sun still shines and love outlasts death – "Grief finds its good way home" and "I have lost my loss."'

THE MAN WATCHING

I can tell by the way the trees beat, after
so many dull days, on my worried windowpanes,
that a storm is coming,
and I hear the far-off fields say things
I can't bear without a friend,
I can't love without a sister.

The storm, the shifter of shapes, drives on
across the woods and across time,
and the world looks as if it had no age:
the landscape, like a line in the psalm book,
is seriousness and weight and eternity.

What we choose to fight is so tiny!
What fights with us is so great!
If only we would let ourselves be dominated
as things do by some immense storm,
we would become strong too, and not need names.

When we win it's with small things,
and the triumph itself makes us small.
What is extraordinary and eternal
does not want to be bent by us.
I mean the angel, who appeared
to the wrestlers of the Old Testament:
when the wrestler's sinews
grew long like metal strings,
he felt them under his fingers
like chords of deep music.

Whoever was beaten by this Angel,
(who often simply declined to fight),
went away proud and strengthened
and great from that harsh hand,

that kneaded him as if to change his shape.
Winning does not tempt that man.
This is how he grows: by being defeated, decisively,
by constantly greater beings.

Rainer Maria Rilke
(translated by Robert Bly)

Chosen by **John Welwood PhD**, clinical psychologist, teacher, Associate Editor of *The Journal of Transpersonal Psychology* and author: 'This poem, in its beautiful translation by Robert Bly, describes the gritty, existential side of the spiritual journey. The spirit is first alluded to as a great storm that threatens to sweep us away. Rilke then speaks about wrestling with the angel, as an instance of "being defeated, decisively, by constantly greater beings". I love the tone and language of this poem – "immense storm", "sight", "domination", "triumph", "bent", "sinews", "beaten", "strengthened", "harsh hand", "kneaded", "defeated" – because they speak of the real challenges of spiritual growth, which some teachers have described as a "path of greater and greater disappointment", until at last you finally give up and let go. This is not the romantic, New Age view of spirituality where everything is all love and light, but the real thing.

'My own journey has involved a great deal of wrestling with the angel. And I think we need to appreciate this as a valid way of coming to terms with the ultimate, of learning to live in accord with what is beyond the human, yet in a human way – in Martin Buber's terms, "to be humanly holy".'

THERE IS A GREEN HILL FAR AWAY

There is a green hill far away,
  Without a city wall,
Where the dear Lord was crucified,
  Who died to save us all.

We may not know, we cannot tell,
  What pains he had to bear,
But we believe it was for us
  He hung and suffered there.

He died that we might be forgiven,
  He died to make us good,
That we might go at last to heaven,
  Saved by his precious Blood.

There was no other good enough
  To pay the price of sin;
He only could unlock the gate
  Of heaven and let us in.

O dearly, dearly has he loved,
  And we must love him too,
And trust in his redeeming Blood,
  And try his works to do.

Mrs C. F. Alexander

Chosen by **Nigel Williams**, author and broadcaster: 'When I sang this hymn at Highgate Junior School about 40 years ago it somehow managed to connect suffering and the English countryside. The Anglicized, sentimental Jesus of my childhood is the only one who means anything at all to me.'

THE WORLD

I saw Eternity the other night
Like a great Ring of pure and endless light,
    All calm, as it was bright;
And round beneath it, Time in hours, days, years
    Driven by the spheres
Like a vast shadow moved, in which the world
    And all her train were hurled;
The doting Lover in his quaintest strain
    Did there complain;
Near him, his lute, his fancy, and his flights
    Wits sour delights,
With gloves, and knots the silly snares of pleasure;
    Yet his dear treasure
All scattered lay, while he his eyes did pour
    Upon a flower.

The darksome Statesman hung with weights and woe,
Like a thick midnight fog, moved there so slow
    He did not stay nor go;
Condemning thoughts, like sad eclipses, scowl
    Upon his soul,
And clouds of crying witnesses without
    Pursued him with one shout.
Yet digged the mole, and, lest his ways be found,
    Worked underground,
Where he did clutch his prey; but One did see
    That policy.
Churches and altars fed him, perjuries
    Were gnats and flies;
It rained about him blood and tears, but he
    Drank them as free.

The fearful Miser on a heap of rust
Sat pining all his life there, did scarce trust
   His own hands with the dust;
Yet would not place one piece above, but lives
   In fear of thieves.
Thousands there were as frantic as himself,
   And hugged each one his pelf,
The downright Epicure placed heaven in sense
   And scorned pretence;
While others slipped into a wide excess,
   Said little less;
The weaker sort, slight, trivial wares enslave
   Who think them brave;
And poor, despised Truth sat counting by
   Their victory.

Yet some, who all this while did weep and sing,
And sing, and weep, soared up into the Ring,
   But most would use no wing.
O fools (said I), thus to prefer dark night
   Before true light,
To live in grots, and caves, and hate the day
   Because it shows the way,
The way which from this dead and dark abode
   Leads up to God,
A way where you might tread the sun, and be
   More bright than he.
But as I did their madness so discuss
   One whispered thus,
This Ring the Bridegroom did for none provide
   But for his Bride.

Henry Vaughan

Chosen by **Colin Wilson**, writer: 'Throughout my teens I think I travelled through a deep sense of meaninglessness and futility – I used to call it nihilism, meaning belief in nothing. Yet there was a deep craving for meaning and for belief. I identified totally with the emotional exhaustion expressed in this poem, and with the hope that, in spite of inability to believe, there might nevertheless be some "salvation".'

A WINTER AND SPRING SCENE

The willows droop,
The alders stoop,
The pheasants group
   Beneath the snow;

The fishes glide
From side to side,
In the clear tide,
   The ice below.

The ferret weeps,
The marmot sleeps
The owlet keeps
   In his snug nook.

The rabbit leaps,
The mouse out-creeps,
The flag out-peeps,
   Beside the brook.

The snow-dust falls,
The otter crawls,
The partridge calls
   Far in the wood:

The traveller dreams,
The tree-ice gleams,
The blue jay screams
   In angry mood.

The apples thaw,
The ravens caw,
The squirrels gnaw
   The frozen fruit.

To their retreat
I track the feet
Of mice that eat
　　The apple's root.

The axe resounds,
And bay of hounds,
And tinkling sounds
　　Of wintry fame;

The hunter's horn
Awakes the dawn
On the field forlorn,
　　And frights the game.

The tinkling air
Doth echo bear
To rabbit's lair,
　　With dreadful din;

She scents the air,
And far doth fare,
Returning where
　　She did begin.

The fox stands still
Upon the hill
Not fearing ill
　　From trackless wind.

But to his foes
The still wind shows
In treacherous snows
　　His tracks behind.

Now melts the snow
In the warm sun.
The meadows flow,
The streamlets run.

The spring is born,
The wild bees bum,
The insects hum,
    And trees drop gum.

And winter's gone,
And summer's come.

The chic-a-dee
Lisps in the tree,
The nuthatch creeps,
    The marmot sleeps;

The catkins green
Cast over the scene
A summer sheen,
    A genial glow.

I melt, I flow,
And rippling run,
Like melting snow
    In this warm sun.

Henry David Thoreau

Chosen by **Paul Winter**, musician: 'Thoreau creates a sound painting of the New England countryside where my soul came alive.'

THE OLD TRUTH

Rumour has it
Once upon a time
Dere was Peace, Luv an Unity
One race, de Human Race etc,
Africans traded wid de Irish
Chinese traded wid de Arabs etc,
Rumour has it,
We made luv in de open.

Before Religion
Before Politricks,
Our names mean someting,
Nu high art,
Nu high brow
Jus a milk an honey scene.

Rumour has it
Jesus   (Peace be upon him)
Krishna   (Peace be upon him)
Mohammed   (Peace be upon him)
Harriet Tubman   (Peace be upon her)
Yim Wing Chun   (Peace be upon her)
Amina   (Peace be upon her)
All came

Rumour has it
Our destinies are all
(Rumour has it)
De same.

Benjamin Zephaniah

Chosen by **Benjamin Zephaniah**, poet and musician: 'I have always respected an individual's personal beliefs and religious experiences. I recognize all the prophets, great and small, but I don't have much time for priests and politicians who manipulate people's religious beliefs for their own gain or for power. The poem says that there are no few – we are all chosen.'

INDEX OF CONTRIBUTORS

INDEX OF POETS

INDEX OF TITLES AND FIRST LINES

First lines are given in italics

[204]